THE IMMIGRANT HERITAGE OF AMERICA
SERIES

Cecyle S. Neidle, Editor

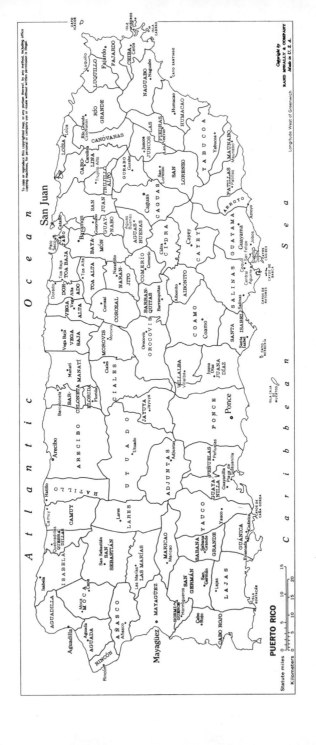

PUERTO RICO

San Juan

Atlantic Ocean

Caribbean Sea

Longitude West of Greenwich

Copyright by
RAND McNALLY & COMPANY
Made in U.S.A.

Statute miles
0   5   10   15
Kilometers
0   5   10   15   20

Puerto Rico and the Puerto Ricans

by

Clifford A. Hauberg

Twayne Publishers, Inc.   ::   New York

Library of Congress Cataloging in Publication Data

Hauberg, Clifford A
    Puerto Rico and the Puerto Ricans.

    (The Immigrant heritage of America series)
    Bibliography: p. 195
    1. Puerto-Rico—History. 2. Puerto Ricans in the
United States. I. Title
F1971.H39   1975   917.295'03'53   74-8812
ISBN 0–8057–3259–4

Contents

About the Author

Clifford A. Hauberg began teaching Latin American history in the Canal Zone schools (Panama) in the early 1940s. He has since taught Latin American history at the University of Wisconsin (summer sessions 1956, 1964) and at St. Olaf College from 1947 to the present. He also served as chairman of the History Department 1969–1971 at St. Olaf. He was visiting professor at the University of Panama during the summer session of 1954, and for the last four years he has taught an interim course at CIDOC (Centro Intercultural de Documentacion), Cuernavaca, Mexico.

Dr. Hauberg has served as consultant and has been the recipient of several grants including the Social Science Research Grant 1952–53. As a result he has traveled extensively throughout Latin America, including a trip to South America in 1969 and a summer sojourn in Bolivia as counselor for SPAN (Student Project for Amity Among Nations) sponsored by the University of Minnesota.

Dr. Hauberg did his graduate work at the University of Minnesota, where he also served as assistant and instructor in the History Department, and received his Ph.D. in 1950. He has published articles in encyclopedias, newspapers, as well as in educational and historical journals. Seven of his articles, treating such countries as Bolivia, Panama, Venezuela, and Guatemala, have appeared in *Current History*. He is the author of *Latin American Revolutions*, published by T. S. Denison Co., Minneapolis, Minnesota, 1968. The preface to his book was written by José Figueres, President of Costa Rica and a world statesman, who comments thus regarding the "awakening of interest" in Latin America which in his opinion was due to pioneer Latin Americanists and "one of these ... is the author ... who teaches Latin American culture with devotion and this devotion is communicated to his students."

Dr. Hauberg is listed in various directories including *Who's Who in Minnesota*, *Who's Who in the Midwest*, *Historians of Latin America in the U.S., 1965* (Howard F. Cline), *Directory of American Scholars*, and *The Dictionary of International Biography*.

Foreword

DR. HAUBERG'S BOOK, *Puerto Rico and the Puerto Ricans* HAS been an extremely enjoyable reading experience for me. Having been born and raised in Puerto Rico, I always look forward to any book that deals with the island, its people, and their accomplishments. There have been times in the past that I have been disappointed—but certainly not in this case, for Dr. Hauberg has brought a sensitive and inquiring mind to the task of recording the plight of the Puerto Ricans, both in the island and on the mainland.

Devoting the first part of the book to giving the reader a clear and accurate view of the island's beginnings—the original inhabitants, the early explorers, the Spanish Conquest and up through the American take-over—Dr. Hauberg offers a very readable and novel-like exposition of Puerto Rican history and American diplomacy in the context of the Old World power struggle in a Caribbean setting.

Once having provided the reader with a clear and unencumbered view of the island's sociopolitical history during the Spanish reign and up through the early years of rule by the Colossus of the North, Dr. Hauberg moves wholeheartedly into an era of time that is of obvious interest to him. It is a chapter in Puerto Rico's history and Part Two in the author's book that is worth reading and rereading. He deals extensively with the two men Rexford Guy Tugwell and Luis Muñoz Marín, who had immense influence in shaping the island's political and economic relationship with the United States. As the author points out, it is significant that in this island of varied ethnic background the two individuals who played the leading roles in shaping the island's destiny, should also be of differing ethnic backgrounds. Fortunate, indeed, was Puerto Rico in having two men of such stature to so dramatically change the island's political and economic direction in a manner that Dr. Hauberg so aptly describes as the "quiet revolution."

That the island's economic problems were deep-set and complex, and not totally removed by the quiet revolution, leads Dr. Hauberg into an in-depth discussion of the "Great Migration" of Puerto Ricans to the North American mainland, and the many problems that they are facing there. It is in this chapter that Dr. Hauberg's extensive research and adept use of data are brought to the forefront, and provide good source material for any student of America's pluralistic communities. In the final pages of his book, Dr. Hauberg offers strong arguments and a solid faith in finding the ultimate solutions of Puerto Rico's problem within the American system of government.

Again, I reiterate, it was an extremely enjoyable reading experience, for Dr. Hauberg brings with him the historian's concern for accuracy and perspective, the social scientist's understanding and interpretation of statistical data, and the novelist's ability to present all of this in a highly readable and absorbing manner.

MICHAEL O'REILLY
Coordinator, Puerto Rican Program
Macalester College
St. Paul, Minnesota

Acknowledgments

THE AUTHOR GRATEFULLY ACKNOWLEDGES PERMISSION GRANTED
by the following companies to quote sections from their books
in this publication: Brown, Wenzell, *Dynamite on Our Doorstep*,
Chilton Book Company, Radnor, Pennsylvania; Lewis, Gordon
K., *Puerto Rico Freedom and Power in the Caribbean*, Monthly
Review Press, 116 West 14th Street, New York, New York;
Hernandez-Alvarez, José, *Return Migration in Puerto Rico*, Uni-
versity of Puerto Rico (Social Science Research Center), Rio
Piedras, Puerto Rico; Hanke, Lewis, *The Spanish Struggle for
Justice in the Conquest of America*, University of Pennsylvania
Press, 3729 Spruce Street, Philadelphia, Pennsylvania; Aitkin,
Thomas, Jr., *Poet in the Fortress*, The New American Library
(NAL), 1301 Avenue of the Americas, New York, New York;
Ramparts, copyright Noah's Ark, Inc., 2054 University Avenue
Berkeley, California; *Newsweek*, 444 Madison Avenue, New
York, New York; Macisco, John J., "Assimilation of the Puerto
Ricans on the Mainland: A Sociological Approach," *International
Migration Review*, Center for Migration Studies, 209 Flagg
Place, Staten Island, New York; Howard, John, *Awakening
Minorities: American Indians, Mexican Americans, and Puerto
Ricans*, Aldine Publishing Company, 529 South Wabash Avenue,
Chicago, Illinois; Castaño, Carlos, The Puerto Rican Migratory
Program," *Makers of America—Emergent Minorities*, Encyclo-
pædia Britannica, William Benton Publisher; Lopez, Lillian,
and Trejo, Arnuefo D., in *Wilson Library Bulletin*, March, 1970;
Wakefield, Dan, *Island in the City*, Knox Burger Associates, 29½
Washington Square South, New York, New York; Senior,
Clarence, *The Puerto Ricans: Strangers—Then Neighbors*, New

Viewpoints, Franklin Watts, Inc., 845 Third Avenue, New York, New York; Rand, Christopher, *Puerto Ricans,* Oxford University Press, 200 Madison Avenue, New York, New York; "Job Plan Helpful to Puerto Ricans", *New York Times,* June 1, 1971; Mathews, Thomas, *Puerto Rican Politics and the New Deal,* University of Florida Press, 15 N.W. 15 Street, Gainesville, Florida; Goodsell, Charles T., *Administration of a Revolution,* Harvard University Press, 79 Garden Street, Cambridge, Massachusetts; Thomas, Piri, *Down These Mean Streets,* Random House, Inc., Alfred A. Knopf, Inc., 201 East 50 Street, New York, New York.

It is impossible to thank all those who have inspired and assisted in the research and writing of this manuscript—individuals as well as institutions. Some, however, merit special mention.

The Office of the Commonwealth of Puerto Rico has been very helpful by contributing significant material as well as ideas. This was true when Jorge L. Cordova was Resident Commissioner as well as after the 1972 election when that function became the responsibility of Jaime Benítez.

Herman Badillo, the first Puerto Rican to be elected to the U.S. Congress, has also been very helpful by furnishing personal data as well as Congressional material.

At the outset of the writing, Drs. Kenneth Bjork and George Sivanich of St. Olaf College read parts of the manuscript and made valuable comments. The author would also like to thank Dr. Samuel Betances, Publisher of *The Rican,* for his criticisms and suggestions.

Michael O'Reilly, Coordinator of the Macalester College Puerto Rican Program, also read the whole manuscript and has contributed pertinent ideas.

Without the assistance furnished by the Rolvaag Memorial Library of St. Olaf College it would have been difficult indeed to have secured all the necessary material.

Lastly, the author wishes to thank two women for their significant assistance. Cecyle S. Neidle, Editor of the Immigrant Heritage of America Series, contributed invaluable suggestions

Acknowledgments

which have been incorporated into the manuscript. Pamela (Kellar) Miller aided in the research, typed, and proofread the manuscript, and her assistance was much appreciated.

CLIFFORD A. HAUBERG

Puerto Rico and the
Puerto Ricans

Part I

Background Factors

CHAPTER 1

Introduction: The Nature of the Problem

THE UNITED STATES ACQUIRED PUERTO RICO[1] AS A RESULT OF THE Spanish-American War in 1898 and "the American flag found Puerto Rico penniless and content." It soon flew over "a prosperous factory worked by slaves" who had lost their lands and could "soon lose their guitars and their songs."

By 1929 the economy of Puerto Rico was dominated by several large absentee-owned sugar estates, and in the words of Muñoz Marín it was a "land of beggars and millionaires, of flattering statistics and distressing realities ... Uncle Sam's second largest sweatshop."[2]

It is significant to point out, however, that by the 1950's conditions had changed, largely due to the role played by Muñoz Marín in Puerto Rican affairs. Puerto Ricans were playing guitars in their homeland and in New York. Moreover, Muñoz Marín was considered by many a friend of the United States, and his "Operation Bootstrap" has been viewed as the proper kind of revolutionary change.[3]

There is widespread ignorance in the United States as well as in Puerto Rico regarding that small island's history and recent revolutionary activity. Undoubtedly many children of Puerto Rico have been brought up on the idea that the great contributions to civilization have been made by well-known colonial leaders—especially English, French, and American. What has transpired in Puerto Rico since the 1940's as a result of Operation Bootstrap is of universal significance. It has come as the result of cooperation between Puerto Ricans and Americans. The *Boriqueños*[4] are probably tired of being stereotyped as weak,

[1]

and rather worthless. There is much to be proud of in the history of Puerto Rico—past as well as present.

Americans,[5] moreover, should be willing to evaluate frankly the colonial period (1898–1930) when the island was ruled in a manner which Justine Whitfield Diffie and Bailey W. Diffie have labeled "A Broken Pledge."[6] However, what has happened since Rexford Guy Tugwell was appointed Governor (1941) might well make many Puerto Ricans proud. The present volume is dedicated to a clarification of the various aspects of Puerto Rico's significant story.

Since 1952 the Puerto Rican flag, a single white star on a triangular blue field with three red and two white stripes, has shared the trade-wind breezes with the United States flag.

Once an outright colony, Puerto Rico is now called Estado Libre Asociado (Associated Free State), which is akin to commonwealth status. Puerto Ricans have been United States citizens since 1917, but unless they have legal residence on the mainland they cannot vote in the United States elections, including the presidential. They do not pay federal taxes but must serve a commander-in-chief in whose choice they have no voice. Puerto Ricans do elect their own governor, as well as a resident commissioner who represents them in Washington—but he has no vote. Moreover, many of the island's significant activities are under federal (U.S.) control—including the post office, radio and television licensing, as well as the customs service. These inconsistencies furnish propaganda for the independence movement, which has had a very small following but is becoming increasingly influential.

Recently, for example. the *New York Times* (March 12, 1971) reported rioting on the Rio Piedras campus of the University of Puerto Rico. There was destruction of property, three people were killed, and sixty were injured. The article evaluated the incident thus:

What remains is the underlying issue in the rioting—the status of Puerto Rico, the question of whether the island is to remain a commonwealth with its special relationship to the United States, or become a state, or become an independent republic.

The article adds: "In the context of Puerto Rican politics, R.O.T.C. is opposed not so much because it trains youth for war but because it is a symbol of the United States' presence" —in other words, a vestige of the old United States imperialism of the Broken Pledge period after 1898. At an earlier stage this issue was even more bitter, as can be seen from the following colloquy:

I remembered this Negro. The last time I had seen him was down at the docks; he was haranguing a group of dock-wallopers.

"You are hungry. Why? Because the Americans starve you. You are idle. Why? Because the Americans will not give you work. Your people die on the streets. Why? Because an American says they shall die. Rise against the American bastards. Obey the dictum of our Master, Albizu Campos. Sharpen the knife which will touch the heart of an American."

These were the words this man had yelled. Now his little beady eyes flicked up at me from time to time, and I wondered if there was going to be trouble. I finished my drink and went to the door. The downpour had not diminished. The street leading to the town was covered with swirling water. I turned back to the bar and ordered another coke. A lean ferret-faced man slid up alongside me.

"You an American," he stated.

"Sí," I agreed and started to invite him in halting Spanish to have a drink.

"All Americanos are sons-of-beeches," announced the man. Then carrying his logic through. "You is Americano. You is son-of-beech. What you say to that, Americano son-of-beech?"

There wasn't anything to say; I kept on sipping at my drink. The *colmado* had gone quiet now, tense and waiting.

The thin man brought out a knife. He tested its edge on a hair from his arm.

"I do not like Americanos." He placed the knife against my stomach. "Maybe you no like Puertoriqueños," he suggested hopefully.

The knife drew blood through my shirt. Other men were gathered about. Their faces showed only glee at my predicament. The big Negro shuffled forward, his face expressionless.

"Well, this is it," I thought.

The Negro's arm leaped out and struck the other man's wrist. The knife clattered to the floor.

"Leave him alone, Pedro." Then turning to the others, he added in Spanish, "What Pedro says is right. All Americans are bastards. But this one is our friend." To me: "Come sit down, we will have stick together. We are all friends here. My name is Gerónimo Notiz. I am the uncle of Jaime. He is your pupil."

Silently I blessed Jaime.[7]

This selection from Wenzell Brown's *Dynamite on Our Doorstep* indicates how colonial arrogance and despair, resulting from never-ending poverty and loss of hope, can bring forth a virulent xenophobia. This has been characteristic of the independence movement in Puerto Rico. Brown's book is an example of enlightened commentary and understanding. Since it was written, a significant change has taken place and mass poverty has been greatly alleviated. Now there seems to be more hope in the island, but the best means of achieving identity for the Puerto Ricans is uncertain. Undoubtedly this calls for the kind of enlightenment displayed by the hero-school teacher of *Dynamite on Our Doorstep*.

As a colony of Spain Puerto Rico was plagued by problems, and also after 1898 when she came under the wing of the United States. It is expected that problems—economic, social, and political—will continue whether the island remains an Estado Libre Asociado, or becomes a state of the union, or an independent republic.

In the first place, it should be pointed out that Puerto Rico is a small island; the smallest of the group known as the Greater Antilles of which Cuba, Hispaniola, and Jamaica are the largest. The 1970 census reported almost three million people living on 3,435 square miles. This makes for a population density of over 800 per square mile and well over 2,000 if one considers only cultivated land. Horrified demographers have often pointed to it as one of the worst examples in the world of the "population explosion." In this connection it should be stressed that over a million Puerto Ricans have migrated to the mainland, largely to New York City, undoubtedly mitigating the problems of the island.

According to geographical surveys roughly 55 percent of the island's surface lies between sea level and altitudes up to 500 feet.[8] Most of this desirable terrain is found on the north coast; it constitutes a plain stretching from Aguadilla on the west to Luquillo on the east—a level strip, one hundred miles long and five miles in width. Here lies 13 percent of the island's land area; it contains half of the urban population, including San Juan, the capital, with 455,421 inhabitants according to the 1970 census.[9] Here too is found about one-half of the island's income as well as approximately 40 percent of the commercial and industrial activity. Most of the island's tourist facilities are centered in and about San Juan.

Very early in its history Puerto Rico acquired a reputation for poverty. The *conquistadores* were attracted by gold but these deposits soon gave out, most of the Taíno Indians who mined it, fled or died, and the conquerors moved on to more fertile fields in Mexico and Peru. Since then the island has been cursed by colonial exploitation and overpopulation. Until 1940, for example, the little country was dismally poor and it had a poor image. This conception was enhanced further by the so-called determinism group of geographers.

In 1936, for instance, a distinguished member of the Huntington school taught at the University's summer session. In the seminars he apparently preached that the tropics rob people of energy and that such regions could never progress without proper guidance and direction from the energetic men of the "temperate" zones.[10] On closer examination it would appear that the "climate" of colonialism rather than its tropical situation has been responsible for many of the social ills of the island— as well as of other exploited regions both north and south. We need only mention the Chicanos in the United States who live as far north as Oregon and Minnesota.

The problem in Puerto Rico, then, has been not only overpopulation and lack of resources but underdevelopment and selfish exploitation as well.

The island has an abundance of crops and some fertile land. In pre-Columbian days the Indians cultivated corn, yucca, sweet potatoes, yams, peanuts, pineapples, guava, tamarind, and papaya as well as other more rare and exotic products. Many crops now considered native were brought from other continents, including sugar cane, bananas, plantains, oranges, lemons, grapefruit, and coffee. The key crops of the most recent past have been sugar (with its significant byproducts rum, molasses, and bagasses), coffee, tobacco, and fruits. Conditions have now begun to change and other economic activities are replacing agriculture as a source of income.

The Puerto Rican climate, considered a liability by the Huntington school of thought, is now looked upon as an asset. Another asset is the island's natural beauty—"the nearest thing to paradise a man will ever see."[11] As a result, tourism has increased considerably, especially after restrictions were placed on travel to Cuba. In the late 1960's income from this source exceeded 200 million dollars, even surpassing that of agriculture. The magic pace of the change is startling indeed. Over 500,000 automobiles of the island are hired by travelers from Florida, New York and California. The tourist as well as Juan (John Doe) buys his gas at Mobil and Gulf, shops at Sears, and probably watches television programs featuring Perry Mason and Johnny Carson.

Because old concepts die hard—the inertia of ideas—the island is still suffering. Puerto Rico has deposits of copper, iron, manganese, cobalt, nickel, titanium, and recently a billion dollar lode of copper ore was apparently discovered in the mountain country of the northwest, near Adjuntas. Despite booster-spirit headlines for several years, many still express doubt as to the possibility of such potential affluence. Seemingly the people find it difficult to adjust their thinking to the status of success and wealth. This should not be hard to understand. For centuries this island people has battled against the grim realities of nature as well as against selfish colonialism. Demographers are wont to say, for example, that decent living standards require two and one-half acres of arable land per person. Whereas the United States has more than three acres per capita, Puerto Rico has approximately three persons for every acre of such land.[12] This circumstance tends to make recent progress and the new spirit in Puerto Rico even more remarkable.

As the population grew, the forests disappeared, especially during the nineteenth century. By 1950 only nine percent of the country was forested. Strict conservation measures have resulted in a comeback; possibly 20 percent of the land is now forested.

Especially interesting is the new utility of the "yagruma" tree. Once regarded as an eradicable pest, it is now prized. Its large leaves are green on top and white on the bottom and were occasionally seen on sale in New York as tropical curios. Because of its two colors Puerto Ricans often used "yagruma leaf" as a descriptive term for a two-faced person. A few years ago a factory was established near Ponce for macerating the wood of the tree which is light and of considerable strength. This synthetic lumber is easily worked, and is fire and vermin proof.[13] It is an excellent example of how to make the most of a disadvantage.

Immediately north of Puerto Rico is what is sometimes called Bronson's Deep, where the ocean bottom plunges down some 27,000 feet.[14] Measured from the bottom this would make the mountains of Puerto Rico the highest in the world, approximately 31,500 feet. Because of this cold, deep water, Puerto Rico has not been noted for commercial fishing. Puerto Ricans do consume large quantities of fish, however, especially *bacalao*, dried, salted codfish. The island's coasts are also noted for saltwater sport fishing, including blue marlin, Allison tuna, dolphin sailfish, arctic bonito, snook, wahoo and others.

More significant, however, is the development of tuna canning in several plants near Ponce and Mayaguez. Until the 1950's most canned and consumed tuna in the United States was caught in the region of the Galapagos Islands and processed on the

Pacific Coast. In 1953 a tuna fish cannery was established at Ponce, and was soon followed by others. The Galapagos Islands are closer to Puerto Rico than to California, and water transportation to Puerto Rico (despite Panama Canal charges) is cheaper than via water to California and rail charges in the United States. The several canning companies, now in successful operation, indicate that "determination" rather than geographic determinism is the decisive factor in such movements as Operation Bootstrap.

But who are these three million-odd people who inhabit the island? Possibly "patchwork" is an apt description of the racial mixtures that live on the islands of the Caribbean, a land area equivalent to the state of Wyoming. Here for centuries came a broad spectrum of racial types including Orientals, Negroes, and Caucasians. In Trinidad, for example, one might hear such terms as mulatto, quadroon, octoroon, mustee, and even mustifino.[15] Although Puerto Rico likes to consider itself unique and different, Gordon K. Lewis concludes:

> There came from the beginning every type of European adventurer, eager to obtain a share of the legendary spoils of the New World, and in the case of the non-Spaniard, to despoil the hated Spaniard of his Catholic empire . . . The Welsh Royalist, the Dutch Jew, Cromwell's transported Irish prisoner, the obscure Spanish soldier, the Puritan merchant-adventurer, the Catholic friar—all crowded into a society of brutal vigor . . .[16]

Like the other islands of the Caribbean, Puerto Rico is a melting pot of racial types, but the people of the island like to consider themselves different and ethnically distinct. They do share a common Hispanic background with their Spanish-speaking neighbors in Cuba and the Dominican Republic. Moreover, in recent years the greatest factor for the change in Puerto Rican identity has been the migration to the United States. Possibly one-fourth of the island's population has lived in the United States at one time or another. It is also significant that some racial surveys in New York place Puerto Ricans in a category apart from whites and blacks.

The Caribbean, however, is a region only in a geographical sense. Puerto Rico, for example, does only about two percent of its business with its Caribbean neighbors. Most of the remainder is, of course, with the United States.

Puerto Rico benefits from the entire Caribbean, like Latin America in general, having become front-page news, especially since 1959, when Fidelismo broke upon the Western Hemisphere. Ex-Governor Muñoz Marín of Puerto Rico, Dr. Cheddi Jagan of Guyana, and Dr. Eric Williams of Trinidad have international reputations. This, of course, makes the Puerto Rican revolutionary movement more significant for that little island and the world. What changes will the future bring? Will Puerto Ricans achieve a satisfactory identity, individual and collective, through independence, statehood, or a modified commonwealth?

CHAPTER 2

Colonial Legacy: Largely Spanish

A RECENT PUBLICATION OF THE OFFICE OF THE COMMONWEALTH of Puerto Rico used the term *microcosmos* to describe that little island's image in a world of tension and controversy. In its struggle for identity it has probably faced all the problems of the exploited colonial regions of the world, as well as the colonial aspects of some of the sovereign states, such as the United States.[1] In this sense its history is not strictly Spanish but rather universal.

The island has served as a sort of social laboratory for the study and testing of contrasting theories, doctrines, and ideas in a twentieth-century world milieu. But it all started with the Indians. Then came the Spanish *conquistador*, but as we have already indicated he was "assisted" by other groups and individuals.

Inasmuch as the early conquerors played an important role in the colonial background and as such contributed to the social milieu that is today's Puerto Rico, the classic description of these men seems to be pertinent:

In the sixteenth century, before the English were able to establish so much as a single successful colony, the Spaniards traversed almost the full extent of those lands which have remained Spanish American, together with other territories now part of the U.S. Their expeditions and conquests were so far-reaching, so spectacular, and withal so romantic, however material their aims, and the men who made them were so remarkable for their audacity, courage, physical endurance, patience in misfortune, and unfailingly optimistic hopes, that some distinctive characterization has seemed to be necessary to set off this period from the more prosaic ages. Hence it has become customary to refer to it as the "era of the *conquistadores*," using the Spanish word for "conquerors" to lend flavor to the expression. The *conquistadores*, in the name of Spain, sought wealth for themselves—easy wealth, sudden wealth, fabulous wealth. The unknown lands of the Americas were the "stock market" of Spanish hopes, to which, however, they gave of their effort and very lifeblood infinitely more than the general run of swivel-chair fortune seekers of the present day. And, despite sordidness, violence, almost the full gamut of evil human passions, they left behind them a picture of themselves which is admirable in the main, attractive, and interesting beyond compare.[2]

In the colonial environment the Spanish privateer and his counterpart, the corsair—Dutch, French, or English who raided and intermingled along the coast—also play an important part. The Latin American wars of independence brought Spanish loyalists from Tierra Firme. And, as the sugar economy developed, slaves were utilized by a veritable rainbow spectrum of nationalities and racial types, including Welsh, Scottish, Irish, Lebanese, and Italians. In the nineteenth century even Chinese coolies were brought in to spice the human stew—all such intermingling substantiating Fray Bartolomé de Las Casas' concept that "all the peoples of the world are men."[3] But let us consider some aspects of the early period in more detail.

Hubert Herring, in writing of the early American Indian, states, "The story ... must be written with soft chalk, easily erased and corrected."[4]

Despite the numerous recent anthropological studies, such caution still seems to be necessary. B. W. Diffie, writing on Puerto Rico about 1930, indicated that the Indian population had once been estimated at 60,000. Writing later, and more carefully about the Indian population in general, the same author emphasizes the danger of exaggeration and concludes that Puerto Rico like Cuba had a total pre-conquest population of "not more than a few thousand naked and half naked people." A recent writer, apparently basing his estimates on current scientific findings, places the figure at 30,000. Somewhere between several thousand and 30,000 would seem, then, to be an educated guess.[5]

Prior to the coming of the Spaniards two tribes (subcultures of the Arawaks), the Arcaicos and the Igneris, had invaded Puerto Rico from Florida, Cuba, and Venezuela respectively. These in turn were conquered by the Taínos, members of another subculture who were dominant when Columbus landed on Boriquén, November 19, 1493, and named it San Juan Bautista.[6] Boriquén was ignored for a time as the Spaniards were more concerned with Hispaniola, Cuba, and regions farther west, in response to rumors that more gold was to be found there.

The Taínos were more docile than their cannibalistic cousins, the Caribs, and were ill-prepared to fight the Spaniards or to defend themselves against the Caribs. They possessed only primitive weapons such as bows, arrows, and wooden swords. Consequently, they were subdued and controlled rather easily by the conquerors.

In addition to cultivating certain native crops already mentioned, these people could boast of other accomplishments. Their houses, built of wood and thatch and usually located near water, were called *bohios*. They had also achieved the *hamaca* (hammock) which was woven from cotton fibers and used for relaxation and sleeping. Women did most of the menial labor while men fished and hunted. Their tools consisted of hooks, nets, and fish traps, but narcotics were also used to stun and thus catch the fish. Men smoked and used tobacco in the form of snuff. As a result of their way of life and their various contributions, some Indian words have found their way into the English language such as *canoa* (canoe), *tobaco* (tobacco), *sābana* (savanna), and *maiz* (maize or corn).

In 1508 Nicolás de Ovando, Governor of the West Indies, decided that Ponce de León should colonize the island which was then called San Juan. That dauntless conquistador set sail August 12, 1508, for the fair land, where he was received by the main *cacique* (Indian chieftain) of the island. After gathering a small amount of gold, Ponce ordered crops planted and returned to Hispaniola with his Indian guest, the chieftain Agüeybana.

In March of the next year, 1509, Ponce returned to the island to begin colonization in earnest.[7] Cattle and horses were introduced and mining was started. By the autumn of 1510 a small gold smelter yielded 100,000 pesos. Also the *encomienda,* which could be described as colonial "welfare," was started. Groups of Indians were placed in the care of Spanish colonizers who were to Christianize their charges and, theoretically, care for them. Significantly, the Indians were expected to work in the mines and do other tasks. As the system developed it might more properly have been termed a form of slavery. It caused the Indians to migrate to other islands, to hide out in the interior and to rebel.[8]

At this time (1510) Ponce also founded the first settlement, Caparra, among the low hills lying west of what today is the San Juan harbor. He also sent for his wife and children; they came to live in a large house which also served as a fortress and his headquarters. In 1511 Caparra's name was changed to Puerto Rico, and in 1521, to improve trading facilities, the town was moved to a small island where Old San Juan now stands. Gradually the capital came to be San Juan and the island, Puerto Rico.

From 1511, which marks the first attempt at resistance by the Taínos, warfare and other troubles plagued the Spanish settlements. Warlike Caribs attacked and pirates sacked and burned along the coast. In 1519 many of the Indians, as well as Spaniards, died of smallpox. By 1530 the small deposits of gold were almost exhausted and so were the Indians. A census of the San Juan area at that time indicated a count of only 426 Spaniards, 1,148 Indians, and 2,077 Africans. This number did not include young children and Indians who had fled to the mountain interior. Gradually the original Indian culture was being liquidated by the abuses and changes wrought by colonialism.

As rumors came back regarding the fabulous riches of the mainland, especially the Inca region, Puerto Rico suddenly seemed rather drab and uninteresting. The popular theme for the gold-hungry Spaniard became "May God take me to Peru!"

Politically, Spain was possibly the best equipped of the budding European nations to acquire and control a colonial empire. For approximately six centuries it had been occupied with the expulsion of the non-Christian Moors (*La Reconquista*). During this period it had built up the machinery to conquer, control, and exploit. This process resulted in the territorial unification of Spain as well as in the development of an absolute form of government, culminating in the strong Machiavellian rule of *Los Reyes Católicos,* Ferdinand and Isabella. Their marriage in 1469 led to the creation of a nation-state, Spain.

During this period such useful machinery as *adelantado* (military governor), *ayuntamiento* (city council), *corregidor* (king's representative), *encomienda* (allotment of conquered people), viceroy (king's other self), and the *audiencia* (royal court) served to control the Moors as well as the Jews. It was comparatively easy to transfer all these elements to the New World. They could be and were used to found cities, mine gold, and enrich the Crown as well as the conquistadors.[9]

Inasmuch as it has been said that "No other single influence is so important in the history of Latin America as the Church,"[10] another aspect of the Reconquista needs emphasis. In the eighth century, when Christian warriors gathered around "King-Arthur-type" leaders such as Pelayo of Asturias, fighting was done in the name of the leader (the king) and the Church (the Lord). Thus gradually a truly significant symbiosis developed, which was enhanced by the widely told story claiming that a star had appeared over the newly discovered tomb of the Apostle James the Greater.[11] This phenomenon was, of course, interpreted as an omen from on high that the Lord favored the champions of orthodoxy. Thus arose the significant war cry, *Santiago y a ellos!* (Saint James up and at them!) which Christian conquerors used as they battled Moors and later the Indians in Mexico, Peru, and Puerto Rico. The get-rich-quick conquistador fought with the sword and swore by the Cross.

Because the Moors and Jews were artisans, merchants, and laborers this symbiosis does much to explain the nature of *dig-*

nidad, Spanish elitism. The clergy, owners of large estates, as well as the *ricos hombres* and *caballeros* thought they had been granted special prerogatives and the God-given right to dominate others. The Old-World shout "Santiago" spurred conquerors on as they massacred Aztecs and Incas. It is undoubtedly significant that Latin America soon became dotted with the place-name Santiago. Somehow Puerto Rico forms an exception. As one scans a map of the island, no major city by that name appears. Possibly there wasn't enough gold there to justify such a baptism.[12]

The colonial political history of Puerto Rico may be divided into two periods: 1) The period of discovery and conquest through the eighteenth century, when Spanish colonial policies were in full sway, and 2) the nineteenth century, when that island, like other areas imbued with the revolutionary ideals, was struggling for more autonomy.

In the early period the Spanish government through the Council of the Indies (created fully by 1524) ruled Puerto Rico in an absolutely paternalistic fashion. Ponce, for example, had the title *adelantado* (advance military governor), and later rulers were termed governors. One of the weaknesses of the Spanish system was that power was shared by so many officials: Church (bishop and archbishop); political state (viceroy, *adelantado,* governor, *corregidor,* and the *audiencia*); economic state (the *Casa de Contratación*), which, theoretically, was under the Council but was really independent. This in turn led to a lack of centralized responsibility and to much delay. Laws were codified in the interest of the people, including the Indians, but often the governor followed the policy of *Obedezco pero no cumplo* ("I obey but do not enforce").

Possibly the situation in Puerto Rico was more extreme because that island was especially valuable strategically. Early it acquired the reputation of being both the cockpit and shield of the Caribbean and the Greater and Lesser Antilles. Here, imperial domination was justified in the view of the Crown, for example, because of the danger from hostile Caribs, French, Dutch, and English pirates and privateers. As a result, Puerto Rico was labeled a sort of "Christian Rhodes," by one early San Juan official. Those in control were more concerned with establishing strong fortresses, La Fortaleza and El Morro, than with agricultural and other civic development. One can hardly blame those in power when it can be pointed out that El Draque (Sir Francis Drake) attempted to take San Juan in 1595, and in May of 1598, George Clifford, Earl of Cumberland, actually possessed "the keys to all the Indies" for a time. The situation was so desperate in the sixteenth century that the Council of the Indies created a *situado*, which was an annual contribution from Mexico for the maintenance of Puerto Rico's military establishment.

Although it is remarkable that the island was successful in fending off these attacks, the lower elements of Puerto Rican society did not benefit. Gradually, two distinct classes developed: 1) the *jíbaros* (rustics) of the interior and the unprotected classes of the seaboard areas; and 2) the military elite of San Juan. Moreover, the concatenation of various forces—war, conquest, slavery, and selfish mercantilism—caused the civilian aspects of society to be subordinated, especially during the early colonial period. This might be illustrated by the remarks of one governor who stated: "A people that was entertained would not indulge in conspiracy." Another thought the island population could be adequately governed with "a whip and a violin."[13]

Probably the kindest thing to say about the Spanish brand of mercantilism was that it was unintelligent. This remark may not be fair because certain aspects of mercantilism have lingered on—even after Adam Smith's *Wealth of Nations* became the "Bible" of free enterprise. Moreover, mercantilism was practiced by all the emerging nation-states of Europe. In the case of Spain, however, the economic system was, because of its *dignidad* (elitism), a system definitely weighted in favor of the Crown and the upper classes. In the long run it defeated its own purpose by furthering exclusivism in profit-making.

First it should be stressed that the statism emerging from feudal Europe stressed bullion wealth as the mark of a prosperous and strong nation. If the individuals of a nation could not mine or steal gold, then it should be acquired by a favorable balance of trade. This system was extremely nationalistic and resulted in a constant state of cold and hot war.

Under the system, colonies were, of course, manipulated for the benefit of the mother country. The *Casa de Contratación*, similar to the English Board of Trade, was created to control Spain's overseas colonies in the interest of the Crown and those running the system. This resulted in royal monopolies, control taxes, special ports for trade and the *flotas* (fleet system). The whole organization was so restrictive and taxes so high that smuggling resulted and outsiders benefited. Possibly the best way to explain the self-defeating nature of the system is to follow a pinch of cotton brought from Chile to a fair at Porto Bello, Panama, and then to Spain in the *galeones* (ships). Here it was sold to a Ghent merchant, and after another long trip it was carded, spun, and woven. The cotton finally returned to Chile by the same route but now a pennyworth of cotton had become a two-dollar handkerchief.[14] Common sense, however, prevailed over this system. The lower classes learned to make their own handkerchiefs and almost everything else. Only the rich used imported merchandise. Smuggling took care of many other wants. But just how did this work out for Puerto Rico?

In the first place it should be stressed that the Spanish settler in Puerto Rico was not a tiller of the soil. He came as a founder of cities or a Crown officer. Moreover, the strategic value of Puerto Rico was considered the most important factor by the Crown. For a brief period Puerto Rico served as a crossroads and San Juan was a bustling port—forty-seven ships called there in 1527. Soon, however, it was being bypassed and the fleet system designated such places as Havana, Cartagena, Porto Bello, and Vera Cruz as terminal cities. In 1662 the governor complained that years had passed without the arrival in San Juan of a single Spanish merchant ship. In 1765 the total exports of San Juan were valued at only 117,000 pesos. However, other merchantmen flying the Dutch, Portuguese, French, and English flags did arrive. Because of the restrictive Spanish type of mercantilism, legal arrangements for trade were not possible, hence smuggling resulted. While some people in San Juan faced starvation, foreign craft a few leagues away were doing a thriving business. Moreover, Puerto Rico gradually became a hideout for privateers and pirates. This vicious system existed until the beginning of the nineteenth century when the winds of revolution began to instill a desire for change—economic as well as political.

The last century of the colonial period might be characterized by the term "aborted liberalism."

Late in the eighteenth century General Sir Ralph Abercromby tried to repeat the tactics which had partially succeeded under the Earl of Cumberland in 1598. After taking Trinidad with ease early in 1797, he moved on to attack by land the powerful fortresses protecting San Juan. A siege of approximately a month convinced him "that no act of Vigour on our Part—could in any manner avail." Abercromby's was the last serious attempt by any European power to take Puerto Rico by force. It marks the end of the early colonial period—an era characterized by strong fortresses and domination by the clerico-military segment of society. Unfortunately the power of the fortresses was to be used not only for military purposes but also in order to stifle enlightenment of the early period and to contain the ideas that stemmed from the revolutions of 1775 and 1789.

So much has been written to glorify the exploits of the *conquistadores* that other aspects of the colonial period are often glossed over or avoided. There were "voices crying in the wilderness" for reform of evils integral to the colonial system. Antonio de Montesinos, a member of the Dominican order in Hispaniola, admonished his well-fed hearers in 1511 this way:

"You are in mortal sin . . . for the cruelty and tyranny you use in dealing with these innocent people . . . Tell me," he cried, "by what right or justice do you keep these Indians in such cruel and horrible servitude . . . Are these not men? . . . Have they not rational souls, are you not bound to love them as you love yourselves? . . . Be certain that, in such a state as this, you can no more be saved than the Moors or Turks."[15]

One of the results of this sermon was controversy in Spain itself, and the publication by King Ferdinand of the Laws of Burgos of 1512. This code called for reforms of the *encomienda*— limited hours of work, adequate food and shelter and proper supervision by royal officials. Nevertheless, the old policies continued and the laws were ignored. However, one cannot argue with Montesinos's courage or his noble intent which was recognized by Hispaniola's distinguished son, Henríquez Ureña, when he referred to the moral indictment of the Dominican as "one of the greatest in the spiritual history of mankind."[16]

Other spiritual leaders who expressed reform ideas were Las Casas, and Bishop Juan de Zumárraga of Mexico. The bishop rebuked his friends when they warned him against those foul-smelling fellows: "You are the ones who give out an evil smell according to my way of thinking. . . . These Indians have a heavenly smell to me. They comfort and give me health . . ."[17] Zumárraga strove to establish Indian schools, to suppress branding and the use of Indians as beasts of burden.

The labors of such leaders resulted in further attempts to curb the evil of the *encomienda,* and the New Laws of 1542 were promulgated by Charles I. They constituted a brave move to restrain greedy *encomenderos* in Latin America including Puerto Rico, but they failed miserably before the clerico-military society that had preempted lands and exploited Indians. It was only over two centuries later that fresh stirrings of revolution from France as well as the U.S. brought enlightenment to Latin America and conditions seemed to augur well for Puerto Rico. With the onset of the nineteenth century, such ideas as liberty, equality, and fraternity for mankind were in the air!

The eminent Puerto Rican Arturo Morales Carrión has empha-

sized the significance of this early Christian humanistic thinking and its impact on Puerto Rico and the world of today:

Any human society, if it is well-ordered and productive, must lay
down as a foundation this principle, namely, that every human being
is a person, that is, his nature is endowed with intelligence and free
will. By this he has rights and duties of his own flowing directly and
simultaneously from his very nature, which are therefore universal,
inviolable, and inalienable.

Morales Carrión then stated:

This is one of the great ideas, if not the greatest, that has animated
Latin American civilization. It is as old as the stirring writings of
Bishop Las Casas on behalf of the Indians. It is as novel as the en-
cyclical *Pacem in Terris* from which it is quoted.[18]

In 1809, Ramón Power y Giralt, an enlightened liberal who
possessed forcefulness and integrity, was chosen to represent
Puerto Rico in the Spanish Cortes. After his arrival in 1810, he
presented arguments in favor of social and economic reforms.
Consequently, Spain sent Alejandro Ramírez as *intendente*
(royal officer) to investigate Puerto Rico; he found financial
crisis and commercial paralysis. He instituted reforms, including
the more efficient collection of customs and taxes, as well as the
Cedula de gracias which allowed some free trade after August
10, 1815. It resulted in improvement. The volume of legitimate
trade which amounted to only $269,000 in 1813 exceeded one
million in 1816 and two million by 1818.[19] Like good "boosters,"
current Puerto Rican publications speak of progress and growth
for that period: "The economy expanded without widespread
slavery. By 1850, of 500,000 inhabitants ... only one in 10 was
classified as a slave."[20]
Such a statement must be examined in juxtaposition to other
evidence. Due to the shortage of slave labor as a result of the
clandestine slave trade, a "work book" regime was imposed upon
"free" labor after 1849. Apparently Puerto Rico, no less than
other parts of the Caribbean, could be considered a society of

masters and slaves and the attempt by historians "to portray Spanish Antillean slaveowners as more humane than others must be seen within the light of contradictory evidence. The claim to an allegedly 'humane' policy was made possible by the presence, at least in Puerto Rico, of a large and 'free' but defenseless labor population that the ruling class could use at will."[21]

Despite the liberal ideas which radiated from Europe and America in the nineteenth century, Puerto Rico was changed but little. Distinguished scholars such as B. W. Diffie (*Porto Rico: A Broken Pledge*) and Gordon K. Lewis (*Puerto Rico: Freedom and Power in the Caribbean*) have surveyed the conditions in that island during the nineteenth century. The change was negligible in such areas as internal improvements, including roads and railroads, educational facilities, land distribution as well as ordinary governmental efficiency. Puerto Rico produced individual leaders comparable to Cuba's José Martí, but like Cuba, significant reform was not forthcoming. At each period of liberal activity, 1809, 1823, 1836, 1868, 1896, Puerto Rican leadership preferred to rely upon the strategy of accepting promises from Spain rather than openly challenging the plutocracy of the island.

Relative to nineteenth-century reform movements, two Puerto Rican leaders illustrate, at least partially, the problem of revolutionary change; José Celso Barbosa, representing the *reformista* (reformist) group, and Ramón Emeterio Betances, who represents the more revolutionary type.

Today, July 27 is a Puerto Rican holiday honoring the outstanding Barbosa who was the first Puerto Rican to attain higher education in the U. S., at the University of Michigan. Later he served as a physician on his home island.

After the Sagasta Pact (1897) arrangement was made with Spain, Barbosa became Under Secretary of Education in the autonomous government and in 1900 founded the pro-statehood Republican Party.

Despite the fact that he represented the needs of the lower classes and enjoyed a reputation as a "man of the people," there is little in his record to suggest that he worked primarily in defense of the working class. Moreover, his well-known position on the race question was little more than a battle concluded in the interest of the colored middle-class professional group to which he belonged.[22]

In fact none of the major parties formed after 1900 and up to the 1930's really worked for significant social and economic reform for the *jíbaro* class and often collaborated with American governors in hobbling such efforts.

This has caused the extremists on the left to label *automismo* (autonomy) as *viciado* (vicious) and *"colonialismo con cadena largo"* (colonialism with a heavy chain).[23]

This type of stereotyping is applied not only to Barbosa, but to Luis Muñoz Rivera who was largely responsible for the Sagasta Pact, as well as to Santiago Iglesias Plantín, "father" of the island's labor movement and founder of the Socialist Party there. Despite his significant reforms after the 1930's, even Muñoz Marín is put by some in this category. It has been said, for example, that no island political leader since 1898 has really created a new political indigenous theory. This definitely seems to be true for Muñoz Rivera, Barbosa, and Santiago Iglesias. Reservations should be made for Muñoz Marín, however, who inaugurated a type of populism which could be called participatory democracy.

At the other extreme are found such leaders as Segundo Ruiz Belvis, Eugenio Maria de Hostos—but especially Ramón Emeterio Betances. If Cuba has its *grito de Yara* (cry for freedom), Puerto Rico has its *grito de Lares* (cry for freedom), because Betances was an *auténtico espíritu refracionario al colonialismo*[24] (authentic rebel against colonialism), who claimed that:

Quien quiera comer tortilla tiene que romper los huevos; tortilla sin huevos rotos y revolución sin revoltura no se ven. (Who wishes to eat a tortilla must expect some broken eggs; a tortilla without broken eggs and revolution without disturbance isn't possible.)[25]

As a well-known doctor, Ramón Emeterio Betances did much to alleviate suffering on the island and also to promote liberal concepts, including the abolition of slavery, freedom of speech and press, as well as independence. For these "subversive" ideas, he was forced into exile several times by tyrannical governors. Returning from such exile in 1860, he again proceeded to fight for reform. Governor Felix Maria de Messinas called Betances to *El Moro* (the fortress headquarters) and there the rebel was threatened with hanging for his dangerous activities. Betances's answer to the Governor indicates why he has become a Puerto Rican hero. "Hear me well, General. The night of that day I shall sleep far more peacefully than your excellency."[26]

Again Betances was banished and again he continued his revolutionary ferment. Encouraged by movements in Cuba after 1865, Betances and others raised troops and procured supplies to inaugurate a revolt for independence in Puerto Rico. Secret societies and codes were organized and communicated with such password letters as "l" and "m," signifying *libertad o muerte* (liberty or death). Although Betances was able to supply 500 rifles, some cannon, and a small ship, *El Telégrafo,* the plot was unsuccessful. The ship of Betances was detained at St. Thomas, Virgin Islands, and his arms were embargoed in Santo Domingo. Nevertheless, others assumed leadership in such places as Mayaguez and the small barrio Pezuela de Lares in September of 1868. Here rebels rallied to the theme, "Muerte o Libertad. Viva Puerto Rico Libre," but their efforts failed rather miserably. Historians disagree as to the significance of *grito de Lares.* It has been termed "mere tomfoolery," easily suppressed, and even the work of foreigners.

On the other hand, Corretjer states: "It is necessary, urgent and decisive for the people of Puerto Rico to contemplate Lares because Lares 'es la piedra de nuestra fundación, el alma de nuestra historia—nuestra única bandera de rendición y de triumfo.' (Our foundation stone, the soul of our history—our only banner of triumph."[27]

During the nineteenth century the central issue and problem of Western industrial nations seemed to be the distribution of wealth among themselves. In the twentieth century, the central question undoubtedly must be the distribution of wealth between the have and have-not peoples. Possibly a Puerto Rican solution might serve as a model for the solution of this global problem. Will the answer be reformism or the path of revolutionary violence?

At any rate, in 1968 pro-statehood Governor Ferré proclaimed September 23 as a holiday commemorating the centennial of *grito de Lares,* when a band of rebels in a small mountain town shouted for independence and a republic as "la única ancora de salvación" (the only way to our salvation).[28]

Despite revolutionary leadership and ferment, four centuries of Spanish colonial rule left Puerto Rico with

no banks, no effective circulation of money, only two or three roads, and a bare twenty kilometers of railroad track. It is symptomatic that the first serious attempt to discover and appraise reliable statistical data about population, employment, and general living standards in the island was undertaken and completed immediately after the American conquest, in the form of the remarkable Report of the Island of Porto Rico composed in 1899.[29]

The terrible colonial conditions in Puerto Rico are stressed emphatically in many writings—"the plums of Puerto Rico were plucked on the island and eaten in Spain."

At the end of the first third of the nineteenth century we find Puerto Rico in a lamentable state of backwardness. According to the writings of O'Reilly, Flinter and Abad, there were practically no schools and very few people knew how to read; everyone outside of the two principal towns went barefoot, and all the other towns were towns only in name.

And at the time of the American occupation:

Land was held by about 4 per cent of the people, 96% being landless in a population that was 79% rural. . . . Ninety-two per cent of the children 5 to 17 years of age were not attending school; 77.3% of the population 10 years of age and over were illiterate.[30]

The ineffectiveness of the local liberalism was dramatically emphasized by the fact that as late as 1887 a Spanish captain-general in San Juan could impose upon the island the repression of *componte* (Caribbean term for arbitrary police brutality), including the illegal arrest of the more famous of the liberal leaders and their subsequently being tortured. This year has gone down in Puerto Rican history as the *año terrible* (terrible year). "The supineness of the same liberalism . . . found expression in the curious fact that the leadership of the leading liberal party (*Partido Automista*) expressed their . . . support of the government measures . . .despite the fact that those measures had been motivated in the main by a desire to crush that party."[31]

Previous to the Spanish-American War, the possibility of reform again beckoned as the greatest of Puerto Rico's early liberals, Luis Muñoz Rivera (1859–1916), after ten years of effort, obtained from Spain the Sagasta Pact of 1897 or "Charter of Autonomy." Much is made of this grant because on paper it was rather broad, giving Puerto Rico dominion status and theoretically the right and power to bring about effective change. But it never had a chance to prove itself. One year later American troops landed near Ponce on the south coast and were warmly welcomed by the people who did not realize that a new brand of colonialism was in the offing.

A final evaluation of the Sagasta Pact should point out that Spanish concessions were usually granted under duress. This was true after 1809 when Spain feared invasion of its strategic island from Tierra Firme, and again when conditions in Cuba threatened to involve American public opinion. The thesis, therefore, that the Pact never had a chance must be based on the assumption that Spain would have acted differently after 1897 than it had in the past—once the crisis was over.

Probably it is more apt to conclude that Puerto Rican liberals were forced to

endure the final humiliation of being rescued by the expeditious action of others, in this case the American action of 1898. His struggle against Spanish injustice thus ended not with a bang but a whimper. He thus made it possible for events, as they overwhelmed him, to fulfill the prophecy of those of his countrymen who had earlier observed that Spain would either save Puerto Rico from American penetration, or the United States would save Puerto Rico from the injustices of Spain.[32]

Thus it appears that Spanish imperialism faded reluctantly and ignominiously, chiefly because it was unable, as other empires were earlier, to grant equality to its colonials.

CHAPTER 3

The Caribbean and Manifest Destiny

MOST PEOPLE WHO THINK OF THE AMERICAN TROPICS PROBABLY
have visions of bougainvillaea, flying fish, coffee *fincas,* bananas,
and revolutionary guerillas. More than any others, two events
undoubtedly first brought the Caribbean to the American mind:
the incorporation of the United Fruit Company in 1899 and
the building of the Panama Canal, which began in 1904. However, seminal changes which laid the bases for American concern about the Caribbean occurred much earlier.

Interest in a canal reaches as far back as Charles I (1516–1556)
of Spain; even stout Cortes considered his search for a route
across the Isthmus as one of his major contributions. During the
later "aggressive defensive" period of the Spanish empire, however, the home government didn't seem too eager to cut through
the narrow Isthmus. Possibly it feared that the ambitious English
might in the long run benefit more from the canal than the
declining Spanish—they might even gain control.

With the emergence of the nineteenth century, however, world
conditions were to be much different. Revolution was in the air
and many new republics in South America had broken away from
the mother country. These would be able to make separate agree-
ments with the affluent, powerful countries and individuals of
Europe and the United States. The impact of the Industrial
Revolution also increased the importance of mining, building
of railroads, shipping, and inter-oceanic canals. If one peruses
the diplomatic correspondence passing between, say, New Granada (Colombia) and Great Britain or the United States during
the first half of the nineteenth century, one will find much
mention of the above topics.

[27]

Consequently, the areas were widely explored. Baron Alexander von Humboldt, for example, supplied voluminous reports about his journeys through areas reaching from Mexico to South America. As a result he, as well as the aging Goethe, considered it the obligation of the United States to build an Isthmian waterway, Goethe adding, "Would that I might live to see it!" Undoubtedly the real father of Pan-Americanism, Simón Bolívar, a pioneer in thinking internationally, also had such visions when he prophesied in his famous letter of Jamaica (1815) that

Qué bello sería que el Istmo de Panamá fuese para nosotros lo q' el de Corinto para los griegos! Ojalá q' algún día tengamos la fortuna de instalar allí un augusto Congreso de los representantes de las repúblicas, reinos e imperios, a tratar y discutir sobre los altos intereses de la paz y la guerra con las naciones de las otras tres partes del mundo![1]

Humboldt was not the only one to investigate possibilities. His interest was largely academic, but the others came to survey and to evaluate possible routes all the way from the Tehuantepec Isthmus of Mexico to the Atrato River in Colombia. Hardy British, French, Swedish, German, and American surveyors proposed specific plans for railroads and canals which would link the Atlantic and the Pacific.

The romance of the American tropics is associated with specific changes within the United States. In the 1820's many leaders in this country regarded the Great American Desert as the permanent western boundary of the republic.[2] Fortunately for the United States, there were some men like John Quincy Adams who had dreams of reaching the Pacific. Hence, after the Congress of Vienna, when it appeared that the power-mad empires of Europe might gobble up parts of the fading Spanish empire, the virtuous farmer republic of the North came up with the Monroe Doctrine of 1823.[3] This warned Russia regarding her possible designs on the Pacific coast of North America as well as the rest of Europe in regard to the Caribbean and South America. Inasmuch as British interests happened to coincide somewhat with those of the United States, and Britain possessed a most powerful navy, the hint was not without effect on those (Metternich and his "fire brigade") who wished to "help" Spain regain the colonies which had broken away after 1808.

These American apprehensions were not unfounded, for it can be pointed out that for a century after 1787 the new republic of America had to face the hostility of most European chancelleries. And, although British interests coincided with those of the United States regarding the independence of the new South American republics, John Bull was not averse to an independent Texas. Even liberal prime minister Gladstone favored the Southern Confederacy at the outset of the Civil War.

The westward expansion of the United States naturally tended to increase ambitions and widen horizons. The friction resulting from the Texan war of independence combined with other factors brought on the Mexican War. The treaty of Guadalupe-Hidalgo (1848) secured the Southwest and California for the United States. Two years earlier, by negotiations with Great Britain, the Oregon territory south of the 49th parallel had also become United States territory. After this, the California gold rush of 1849 inspired thousands to cross the western deserts while additional thousands took the Isthmian route to reach the pot of gold at the end of the rainbow. All these events stimulated what has been termed "Manifest Destiny."[4] At first this idea was applied largely to contiguous territory in the spread westward. Apparently, however, the strategic and economic values of the Caribbean region soon convinced the growing republic of the North that Providence had intended the Caribbean eventually to become an American lake.

The first enterprise which indicates the growth of the new trend was the building of the Panama Railroad. Contrary to the usual account in histories of the United States, the first railroad to connect the waters of the Pacific and the Atlantic was not completed at Ogden, Utah, on May 10, 1869, but rather in Panama, on a Sunday, in January, 1855.[5]

As a result of previous surveys, three American promoters,

Henry Aspinwall, John L. Stephens, and Henry Chauncey secured a grant from New Granada (1849) to build a railroad
across the Isthmus of Panama. Great difficulties caused them to
sell their interest to the Panama Railroad Company which was
incorporated in 1850 by the New York State legislature with a
capitalization of $1,000,000. Despite the great difficulties associ-
ated with tropical diseases and tropical rivers that might rise
due to flash floods forty feet overnight, the road was built.
Even before the last spike was driven, the gold-hungry "Forty-
niners" used it part way, and as a result, the road was one-
fourth paid for before completion.

The building of this road is an excellent example of what
might be called "romantic Puritan enterprise."[6] Moreover, it
proved to be extremely profitable in its early years; by the 1860's
it was declaring an annual dividend of over 40 percent. Poor
management compounded by competition from transcontinental
lines in the United States after 1869 caused the rails of the
Panama line to gather rust during the 1870's. In 1878 the railroad
was sold at considerable profit to the French canal company
headed by Ferdinand de Lesseps of Suez Canal fame. After
cursory investigation and numerous French-style celebrations,
the digging started for an Isthmian Canal. But De Lesseps
encountered difficulties that were different from those that had
been met on the sands of the Sinai region. The Culebra cut with
its shifting sides as well as rising tropical rivers created unantici-
pated problems. Moreover, malaria and yellow fever took their
deadly toll. Today on both sides of the Isthmus one may view
the many crosses that mark the graves of laborers and French
officials alike. At that stage science had not yet discovered that
a deadly mosquito, rather than bad air (*mal aire*), was the cause
of the high death toll.

As a result of these difficulties and bad luck, the French
company collapsed in 1889. A new company was formed, however, to liquidate by selling the assets to the highest bidder. This
turn of events, as well as other basic considerations sharpened

by "Manifest Destiny," brought the United States into the canal business.

According to Justice Holmes, truth in history is decided by the "majority vote of that nation which can lick all others."[7] The Spaniards wrote the history of the *conquistadores* in the earlier centuries, but the United States would write the history of the Monroe Doctrine, Pan-Americanism, the Panama Canal, as well as that of Puerto Rico and the *Alianza para el progreso*.

No event illustrates the above concept better than the story of our acquisition of the Panama Canal. More than any other event, with the possible exception of the Spanish-American War, it explains why the United States earned the sobriquet *El Coloso del Norte*.

As a result of these broadened horizons, the United States negotiated the Bidlack-Mallarino Treaty (1846–48), which gave it the right to supervise and control any mode of transit across the Isthmus. It should be emphasized, however, that by this same treaty we specifically agreed to guarantee the sovereignty of New Granada (Colombia).

When the French, under the guidance of De Lesseps, started the bold enterprise, the United States was very concerned. Some leaders even thought the whole affair contrary to the Monroe Doctrine.[8] As indicated, the French company collapsed in 1889 and the United States was, of course, interested in taking over. An increased interest by the United States is understandable in view of the growing importance of the Pacific Coast in the American economy and the strategic implications of the proposed canal. During the United States confrontation with Spain over Cuba the S.S. *Oregon*, using the straits of Magellan, traveled 14,000 miles from California to Cuba. It arrived apparently with "not a bolt nor rivet out of place"—but it took 66 days to complete the trip.

It is not appropriate to discuss here the details of the Nicaragua-versus-Panama controversy. Why, for example, was Panama chosen when the Walker Commission had recommended

Nicaragua? Theodore Roosevelt himself, in writing to his sister, Anna Roosevelt Cowles, had favored that route in 1894.[9]

Suffice it to say that bribes were involved, Machiavellian tactics were used, and by 1900 President Theodore Roosevelt had definitely decided on Panama as his first choice.

In order to clear the way the Clayton-Bulwer Treaty[10] was abrogated and the United States attempted to negotiate the Hay-Herrán Treaty[11] with Colombia. When the Colombians delayed and finally rejected the treaty, Theodore Roosevelt characterized them as blackmailers, jackrabbits—and contemptible creatures.

Furthermore, when the Colombian leaders at Bogotá turned down the American offer, it was natural that the province of Panama should be very disappointed. Moreover, the history of relations between that province and the Bogotá government was one of constant friction. It was therefore not surprising that a small group of leading Panamanians should organize to break away from Bogotá. Considering the implications of Manifest Destiny as well as the character of President Roosevelt, it was not exactly shocking that American ships appeared on the scene in Colón, Panama, November 2, 1903, to prevent Colombian troops from putting down a revolt in their own territory. The Bidlack-Mallarino Treaty had given the United States the right to supervise and control the neutrality of the Isthmian route. It also stipulated that the United States should protect Colombian sovereignty on the Isthmus. In his book E. Taylor Parks analyzes the obligations of the two nations under the Treaty of 1846–48 and concludes that our interference was unwarranted.

Possibly some of the epithets Teddy Roosevelt reserved for Colombians might more properly be applied to Americans interested in the affair.

On November 3, 1903, American power in the zone area prevented Colombian troops from moving to Panama City, but some aides and the military commander were allowed to cross on the railroad. A small military force, a fire brigade of 441 men and a $100,000 bribe did the rest. Until recently the source of the bribe has been a mystery. Stephen Birmingham in *Our Crowd* has apparently solved the riddle. Dr. Manuel Amador Guerrero came to the United States capitol in the fall of 1903 to promote the Panamanian revolution. He in turn made contact with the enthusiastic Frenchman Philippe Bunau-Varilla who was doing everything possible to promote the De Lesseps project over the Nicaraguan route. In meetings between Bunau-Varilla, the Panamanians, and influential U. S. bankers, (Seligmans and others), the bankers wanted to know how much a revolution would cost. The Panamanians thought it would cost 6 million dollars. Bunau-Varilla brought this request to Seligmans who said that 6 million was too high. Bunau-Varilla returned with the best offer of the bankers— $100,000. It had to be a cut-rate revolution!

After this one-act skit of history, the United States recognized Panama as an independent country; *de facto* recognition was granted on November 6—an embarrassingly short tour de force.

On November 18, 1903, the Hay-Bunau-Varilla Treaty granted to the United States a ten-mile strip of the Isthmus in perpetuity for $10,000,000 plus a $250,000 annual payment beginning nine years after the date of ratification. The treaty was approved by Panama and the United States and proclaimed February 26, 1904. For all practical purposes that small country became a satrapy of the United States.

American presence in Panama has brought many benefits to that small country—but also problems and controversies. It is significant that this friction started immediately after the United States assumed power. The situation was similar to that in Puerto Rico and Cuba.[12] It is unfortunate that events associated with the Russian Revolution of 1917, the Cold War, and the Castro take-over in 1959 have blurred the real issues connected with the "revolution of rising expectations."

In order to understand the significance of power in the Caribbean one should trace the history of the Monroe Doctrine. When first stated, December 2, 1823, it had the appearance of altruism, for it appeared to protect the newborn republics south of our border from "the unregenerate," power-hungry empires of Europe. According to President Monroe, the American continents were no longer open to colonization and the political system of the European powers, being despotic, should not be extended therein, as that would be considered dangerous to peace and security. President Monroe enunciated the doctrine of "two hemispheres" by promising neither to interfere with existing colonies nor to meddle in matters pertaining to the European powers.

It is the first of these negative promises which is often ignored or glossed over in the teaching of "story-book" American history. Nevertheless, there are many Americans who have had and still have an abiding faith in the document as though it were sacrosanct. On the 100th anniversary of the statements by Monroe, Mary Baker Eddy was quoted in the *New York Times*: "I believe strictly in the Monroe Doctrine, in our Constitution, and in the laws of God."[13] It should be pointed out, however, that as issued it was not law, neither national, international, or celestial and it wasn't even a treaty or multilateral agreement—merely a unilateral statement relating to Latin America. Moreover, in the period from 1823 to 1845, there was European interference in Mexico, Central America, and the La Plata (Argentina) region, and Britain actually took over the Falkland Islands in 1833. The United States did little or nothing to prevent such intervention.

As has already been pointed out, the Bidlack-Mallarino Treaty marks the change in American attitude as regards the Isthmus; it also indicated that foreign policy is usually based on self-interest and not on altruism. Even before the Mexican War was terminated, Manifest Destiny made control of an Isthmian route desirable.

After the building of the Panama Railroad, the United States became increasingly more preoccupied with Latin America and the enforcement of the Monroe Doctrine.[14] During our Civil War, we protested Napoleon III's attempt to set up an empire in Mexico; and after the war General Sheridan was sent to the border with 25,000 troops. Finally, Maximilian I and his forces were beaten by Juárez near Querétaro and he was shot on the Hill of Bells June 19, 1867.

The strongest interpretation of the doctrine comes later, however, as a result of feuding between Great Britain and Venezuela over the proper boundary between the two countries. Lord Salisbury apparently considered the Monroe Doctrine antiquated and rejected the American offer to mediate. The upshot of the whole affair was a sharp note from Secretary Olney to the British Ambassador: "Today the United States is practically sovereign on this continent, and its fiat is law upon subjects to which it confines its interposition."[15] When Lord Salisbury still refused to bend, the President, fully alive to "consequences which may follow," sent a sharp note to Congress asking for $100,000. Great Britain really had too many serious problems throughout the empire to challenge the United States. The dispute was finally submitted to arbitration.

During the dispute the British leaders, as well as the British public, more or less adopted the enlarged interpretation of the Monroe Doctrine. If the United States insisted on a "hands off" policy by Europe, then it need be "responsible for the petty impetuous little states...."[16]

This is exactly what was happening and later this concept became known as the "Roosevelt Corollary." It is best illustrated by the Panama affair of 1903 and by the Dominican situation at the turn of the century. As a result of the inefficient rule of Ulíses Heureaux in the Dominican Republic, the foreign debt had risen to $32,000,000. Belgium, Italy, and France threatened intervention and President Roosevelt thwarted this by creating a receivership for the wayward derelict, 1904–1907. Marines moved in and the United States supervised the collection of revenues. That the policy was not all bad is indicated by the fact that the 45 percent of the revenue collection allotted to the government was more than the total had been before. Nevertheless, it was a far cry from the original Monroe Doctrine.

Such unilateral action has caused much hostility and criticism, even bitter hatred, which has been expressed in the writings of Latin Americans: "I conclude that the Monroe Doctrine is not a doctrine but a dogma . . . not a dogma but two, to wit: the dogma of the infallibility of the American President and the dogma of the immaculate conception of American foreign policy."[17]

When a nation of virtue prides itself on its democratic and egalitarian heritage it naturally must seek to square its new-found imperialism with its past traditions. The United States differed little from other nations in this respect, except that it possessed a strong Puritan background which demanded moral justification. Hence much was written to justify making the Caribbean an American lake in accord with Manifest Destiny: It was the law of nature to expand, geographical propinquity justified it as a natural right, and the doctrine of the "white man's burden" was also invoked to make it the moral duty to civilize backward peoples. Obviously the two basic reasons for our interest were economic and strategic. Apparently the writings of Captain Alfred Thayer Mahan had as much influence on President Roosevelt as on the German Kaiser, especially when Roosevelt implied that Puerto Rico and Cuba were to the Panama Canal what Malta was to the Suez. When, therefore, Cuba beckoned because of revolutionary activity and Spanish atrocities, American leaders like Roosevelt, Henry Cabot Lodge, Elihu Root, and Albert J. Beveridge (among others) were not averse to completing the process of making the Caribbean an American lake.

It should also be stressed that the Cuban conflagration was a godsend to the yellow press in the United States. William R. Hearst and Joseph Pulitzer were rivals whose papers burst out in "typographical paroxysms" when "outrageous" incidents were reported regarding concentration camps and Spanish brutality. As a result, the general public became so aroused with righteous humanitarianism that it is doubtful if President McKinley could have prevented the war even when Spain accepted all of his ultimatums except that of assuming blame for the sinking of the battleship *Maine*. His war message of

April, 1898, was passed by a large majority of the House (311 to 6). The voice of the people as well as the "will of Almighty God" had been heard.[18] Inasmuch as the original Monroe Doctrine was also associated with Providence and one principle of that policy promised *no interference with existing colonies,* can one look for compliance with the Ten Commandments in foreign policy?

It helped but little, for example, that the Spanish Minister answered American protests concerning Spanish atrocities in Cuba by comparing such incidents with what Sheridan had done in the Shenandoah Valley or Sherman on his terrible march through Georgia during the American Civil War. The Spanish-American War was fought with Spain in 1898 and both Cuba and Puerto Rico came under the aegis of American imperialism by the Treaty of Paris signed December 10, 1898.

CHAPTER 4

American Colonialism: Broken Promises[1]

OVERWHELMINGLY THE PUERTO RICANS WELCOMED THE AMERICAN troops which supposedly meant "freedom" under American leadership. Why not? A great majority of the *jíbaros* probably knew little about the United States; moreover, they had no love for the elitism or *dignidad* of the Spaniards who had oppressed them throughout the centuries. Undoubtedly many knowledgeable Puerto Ricans accepted the American rule uncritically in 1898 because of the glittering ideals associated with our Declaration of Independence, the fame of such men as George Washington and Abraham Lincoln, and our remarkable material success. Moreover, had not General Miles proclaimed very generously:

We have not come to make war upon the people of a country that for centuries has been oppressed but on the contrary to bring you protection . . . to promote your prosperity, and to bestow upon you the immunities and blessings of the liberal institutions of our government.[2]

Unfortunately, the knight-errant, Sir Galahad image of the United States was soon to be tarnished and Puerto Rican high hopes were to be dashed on the rocks of despair—at least for a time.

Possibly the best explanation for this is to be found in a type of blind and bland arrogance that comes with power and affluence; the arrogance of Puritan thrift and self-assurance began to replace Spanish *dignidad* and the swagger of the *conquistador*.

Unwilling or unable to face its new responsibility openly, and reluctant to be classed as imperialistic, the United States caused Puerto Rico to be termed an "unincorporated" rather than an "incorporated" territory, because the latter term implied that the territory would eventually become an American state. Thus, after the Foraker Act of 1900 was passed, the beautiful little island had a flag without a constitution and citizenship without suffrage; also, it became a "state" without representation. Spanish rule had been autocratic; American democratic rule, despite its glowing heritage, was also autocratic.

In the Insular Cases decision the Supreme Court of the United States held that the Constitution does not follow the flag at all times.[3] Puerto Ricans learned that they were denied certain fundamental constitutional rights, such as indictment by grand jury, right of trial by jury, and the usual limitation on the power of congressional taxation. In Downes vs. Bidwell, especially, a distinction was drawn between basic guarantees of the Constitution and the non-fundamental guarantees of Congress. Justice Harlan's minority opinion indicated that "incorporation" possessed some occult meaning difficult of apprehension. The pertinent wit of Mr. Dooley put it more irreverently in summing up the Insular Cases—"abroad states of the Union are states and territories are territories, but God knows what they are at home."[4]

In short, after 1900, Puerto Rico was just what Congress proceeded to make it—a colony.

This thinking (or lack of it) characteristic of early American imperialism is well demonstrated by the statements of President Coolidge relative to Machado's regime in Cuba, as well as by the Puerto Rican dilemma. During the Pan American Congress of 1928 held at Havana, Cuba, President Machado was especially uneasy regarding anti-United States behavior. Also, he was eager to give an impression of Cuban stability. Men engaged in putting up signs were arrested by the Cuban police and never seen alive again. Parts of one were later found in a shark. His coat and cuff links were recognized by his wife, who was thereupon deported, and shark fishing was thereafter prohibited. Meanwhile, Coolidge praised the prosperity enjoyed by Cuba as a result of the "peace and stability" produced by Machado's regime.

At the same time Puerto Ricans were very disappointed at not having a representative at Havana, and not being treated as a sovereign nation. They asked the United States for "the freedom that you enjoy, for which you struggled, which you worship, which we deserve, and you have promised us."[5]

To such questions Coolidge replied via the Governor of Puerto Rico as follows: "The United States has made no promise to the people of Puerto Rico that has not been more than fulfilled, nor has any representative or spokesman for the United States made such a promise."[6]

Apparently Coolidge had heard neither of Theodore Roosevelt's "splendid little war" nor the promise made by General Miles to the Puerto Ricans. Is it any wonder that Puerto Ricans began to look upon the new presbyter as nothing more than the "old priest writ large."

It was only natural that the first rule in the island was military. This was originally set up by General Miles and lasted until 1900, directed in turn by Generals John R. Brooke and Guy V. Henry. Under their leadership reforms were begun which were appreciated by the Puerto Ricans and augured well for the future. Such reforms were a postal system, a police force, the right of trial by jury, and Habeas Corpus, as well as free public schools.[7] Measures were taken to cut down the high disease and mortality rates; however, these efforts lagged somewhat in producing results.

The Foraker Act of 1900 replaced military government with a civilian one and created a political entity termed "the People of Puerto Rico"—neither citizens of the United States nor citizens of an independent state. This act provided for a Governor to be appointed by the President as well as an Executive Council, also appointed. Furthermore, the first organic act stipulated that Puerto Rico should have a 35-member elected House of Delegates as well as an elected Resident Commissioner to represent it in the United States Congress; he could speak, but had no vote. The laws passed by the House of Delegates were subject to the Governor's and Congressional vetoes. In legal matters Puerto Rico was placed under the United States system, specifically the Circuit Court of Boston.

The chief weakness of the act from the Puerto Rican point of view was that it made no provisions for plebiscites and made no mention of Puerto Rico's future status, whether it was to be independence, statehood, or some form of home rule. The precedents for such action were notable, beginning of course with the Northwest Ordinance of 1787. Both Florida and Louisiana had been promised ultimate statehood in the treaties which arranged for their transfer to the United States, and they had received it. When one considers the hopes of the Puerto Ricans, as well as the democratic climate of the United States, and the promise of General Miles, it should be easy to understand the stunned disappointment of the Puerto Rican political leaders.

Moreover, this disappointment seems more significant when the Foraker Act is considered in juxtaposition to the Spanish grant of autonomy—the Sagasta Pact of 1897. The latter charter conceded the right of Puerto Ricans to participate in the negotiation of commercial treaties which might affect their economy. The Spanish pact also gave true representation in the national parliament and stipulated that amendments to the pact would not go into effect without the prior consent of the island's legislature. As noted, the Foraker Act did not provide for Puerto Rican representation in the United States Congress, and the United States Congress retained complete sovereignty in the area of treaties as well as in important amendments to the act.

It is probably significant that the first major change in United States-Puerto Rican relations came under duress, in much the same manner as when Spain was forced to agree to the Sagasta Pact. On the eve of American entry in the First World War, the Jones-Shaforth Act (commonly called the Jones Act) was passed, on March 2, 1917. It greatly extended the rights and powers of the Puerto Ricans. Collective (U.S.) citizenship was granted, although it was opposed in Puerto Rico by the majority Unionist Party, because it was felt to be inconsistent with a demand for independence. The Executive Council was supplanted by an elected Senate. As in the case of the Foraker Act, the executive power was continued strong and rather independent of popular legislative control. For example, two of the most important cabinet officers composing the Governor's Council were still to be appointed by the President of the United States. They were the Commissioner of Education and the Attorney General. In 1927 this act was amended, placing the Auditor in the same category, i.e., appointed by the President by and with the consent of the United States Senate.

After this the two popularly elected chambers tried to enlarge their power within a framework which had been deliberately designed to curb it. The Puerto Rican, accustomed to colonial abuse, accepted a secondary status with patience and some good humor. For a time after 1917 a popular song went the rounds entitled "Bill Jones." But it did not hide the bitterness which swept over them as they contemplated the degradation of their democratic status.[8]

Unfortunately, other factors favored neither democracy nor effective government. The political parties, before as well as after 1917, tended to cooperate with the executive power in hobbling populist movements, which, if encouraged, might have brought on significant reforms. This was true of the Republicans, the Unionists as well as the Alianza after 1924. Moreover, the Resident Commissioner in Washington helped promote the "red scare" panic in the postwar period. Even José Celso Barbosa, labeled "a man of the people," was not too concerned with lower, working-class interests. As a Republican leader he battled more for the colored middle-class professional. Muñoz Rivera was possibly more sensitive to the real needs of the country, but failed to utilize his great personal influence to work out a practical program of reform.

It should also be stressed that the governors appointed by the

President for Puerto Rico left much to be desired. Half of them were former Congressmen or retired military men. All but a few arrived on the scene knowing little or nothing of the island's problems. Theodore Roosevelt, Jr., who held the office from 1929 to 1931, was probably the best-loved of the Broken Pledge (1898–1930) period. He really tried to take full note of the grinding poverty of the *jíbaros* and the generally bad conditions. He wrote and talked in favor of Puerto Rico as a great American asset in hemispheric relations—"a show window looking south." As a mainlander occupying La Fortaleza, he apparently tried to find a solution to the perplexing problems that would undoubtedly accompany both statehood or independence. These early attempts at reform were thwarted by the years of depression as well as political machinations.

Within the framework of the Jones Act, however, democratic ideals and significant investigations of social conditions provided the leaven for change. Probably no political aspect after 1917 of the island's life was more meaningful in that early period than the emergence and growth of the Socialist Party. In the election of 1914 the Socialist Party received only 4,000 votes, in 1920, 60,000, and in the election of 1928, which was hotly contested, it secured 8 of the 19 senatorial seats and 18 of the 39 in the lower house. Apparently the time had come for Puerto Rican as well as American leadership to recognize the challenge arising from a political situation which allowed economic domination to convert Puerto Rico into an island sweatshop.

From the beginning the focus of power was not so much the American Congress, but the pressure and influence exercised by commercial interests—especially sugar. In typical mercantilistic fashion money was forthcoming for "thoughtful books" which espoused the "possibilities of our new possession."

A most striking change took place in agriculture when sugar increasingly became the principal crop, replacing coffee, the latter having enjoyed certain advantages under Spanish rule. Previous to 1898 some 40 percent of the cultivated area was devoted to coffee because the Puerto Rican brand was very popular in Europe. This crop also benefited from Spanish tariff protection. Significant developments reversed these advantages.

In 1899, San Ciriaco, one of the most severe hurricanes of modern times, hit the island, taking a heavy toll of life and property; the damage to coffee plantations ran well into the millions. Destruction of this kind requires up to fifteen years for full recovery; not only are the shrub-like coffee trees destroyed but the necessary shade trees as well.

In addition to this, sugar received tariff protection after 1898 whereas coffee was duty free and had to compete with products from other areas.

Probably the most important factor in bringing about change was that sugar as a crop benefited more than coffee from capitalistic investment in mills as well as in land. Despite the fact that the Foraker Act included a provision known as "The Five-Hundred Acre Law" which made it illegal for corporations to own or control more than 500 acres of land, the sugar industry was soon dominated by four powerful corporations. The law was ignored.[9] They obtained land by purchase, lease, and foreclosure: they also built mills, creating an economy which required seaports, highways, railroads—in short, industrial progress. By 1917 the number of holdings in excess of 500 acres was 477, and the land so held numbered 537,193 acres, with a property value of $36,500,000. Land leased by these same companies totaled 229,000 acres, with a value of $21,000,000.[10] By 1940 the largest of the "Big Four," the Eastern Puerto Rican Sugar Co., managed 54,700 acres of which only 20,900 were planted to cane. The remainder was held in reserve, possibly used for the idyllic pasturing of stock while many *jíbaros* looked on—landless.[11] The nature of this enterprise is one reason why the early American period can be labeled "A Broken Pledge."

A superficial glance at the sugar industry reveals pyramiding production measured in tons and dollars; a veritable cascade of riches and prosperity. But because the industry was owned and controlled by outsiders, the millions made in sugar production give a false impression. The profits were enjoyed by many who never saw Puerto Rico; whereas the wages which in bulk seemed so large were miserably inadequate for the necessities of life.

In Puerto Rico the per diem for sugar cane workers was considerably less than for similar workers in Hawaii and Cuba: 63¢, 97¢, and $1.26 respectively. Throughout the 1920's wages were less than a dollar per day, whereas in Central America and the Bahamas they ranged from $1.25 to $1.95. Due to the seasonal nature of much harvest work, unemployment was also very high, ranging from 17 percent in 1899 to 25 percent in 1920, and reaching 30 percent in 1930.[12] What made conditions even worse was the fact that the profitability of sugar stifled the continued production of food products, rice and corn, both of which had been of considerable importance before 1898.

These developments in turn led to the decline of the small holdings in agriculture. As the sugar industry yielded to large-scale production aided by technological change, the *colono* (farmer) became more and more dependent. Contracts which determined the range of relationships with the owner of the *centrales* (sugar factories), were in favor of the entrepreneur, for the *colono* incurred all expenses of cultivation, including the hazards of hurricanes, and paid high interest rates on money he usually had to borrow from the *central* management. Thus, the smaller type *colono* found himself working against impossible odds. He was obliged to follow one of two courses: either to continue borrowing or sell out. Statistics on mortgages indicate that he usually was forced to take the latter option. This meant the gradual disappearance of the small farmer. It is not surprising that many of the political activities after 1930 came from this segment of society. In 1935 Secretary Ickes could write: "Puerto Rico has been the victim of the laissez-faire economy which has developed the rapid growth of great absentee-owned sugar corporations, which have absorbed much land formerly belonging to small independent growers and who in consequence have been reduced to virtual economic serfdom."[13]

Much the same can also be said of economic activity in such fields as tobacco, fruit, shipping, especially when considered in juxtaposition to items related to the general welfare—wages, prices, taxes, and general living conditions.

The development of the tobacco industry in Puerto Rico has been somewhat the same as sugar. In 1899 only 600 acres were devoted to tobacco production; in 1929 it had expanded to 30,000 acres. Much of this increase was due to governmental encouragement and dissemination of new ideas, including fertilization, destruction of parasites, as well as the use of hybrid seeds and better methods of caring for the harvested product.

The important difference between the development of tobacco and sugar is the failure of the tobacco industry to try to gain control of the land in a manner similar to the sugar corporations. Although possibly 80–85 percent of the tobacco business was in the hands of large companies, the Puerto Rican farmer was offered a rather good market for his product. The following quotation indicates the rather steady growth:

Just how much the cigar export has grown since that time may be seen from the following table which represents the amounts exported in selected years:

1900:	100,000	1920:	223,316,450
1910:	151,724,438	1925:	196,560,000
1915:	174,275,407	1929:	158,780,620

The principal part of the cigar output was consumed at home in 1899, but the export crop is now far in excess of domestic consumption. One factor which encouraged home consumption of cigars in 1899 was the high tariff which practically forbade imports, even from Cuba.[14]

In Puerto Rico, as in Cuba, the field ownership of tobacco did not fall into the hands of the corporations. Therefore, tobacco is termed the poor farmer's product in these countries.

From the viewpoint of Puerto Rican labor, the best of the major crops is fruit. Puerto Rican citrus fruit has three blooms and therefore there is really no dull period. This makes the field work almost continuous; between-the-harvest activities such as pruning, fertilizing, weeding, and spraying furnish almost steady, year-around employment. Moreover, wages in this industry were the highest in the early period. One study by a professor of the University of Puerto Rico shows an annual wage for fruit workers of $217.00 as compared with $183.00 for coffee and tobacco workers, and $207.00 for sugar workers.[15]

The wage situation was even worse when considered in relation to taxation and the tariff. According to the Diffie study, published in 1931, the tariff on principal Puerto Rican foodstuffs raised the total price by approximately $9,000,000 or 30 percent annually. This meant that the average worker who earned 60¢ to 80¢ a day received in value 48¢ and not 80¢. The people of Puerto Rico paid almost four million dollars more for rice than they would if they could have purchased that important item in an open market. The case was similar for all the other basic foods—flour, lard and lard compounds, dairy products, beans, meats, potatoes, peas, corn meal, as well as numerous other items.

In the area of taxation the powerful absentee owners were not only able to have their properties assessed very low but often passed on to the *colono* the taxes meant for the *centrales*. Although Puerto Rico was not completely a "sugar island," as is Cuba or Barbados, it was sufficiently so to prove that sugar cane does not make a colony happy or a people more advanced culturally. Puerto Rico was freed from Spain, but apparently it was necessary to war against the colonialism of sugar and absentee ownership.

In the field of banking and public utilities the story was much the same as in the sugar industry. Absentee ownership controlled about 50 percent of the banking industry and its related activities. As a result, the interest rate ranged from 8 percent to 12 percent or almost twice as high as the United States rate of 6 percent. It has been argued that the danger of Latin American revolutions justified such rates in the Caribbean. Puerto Rico, however, after 1898, could hardly be compared with such regions as Central America, Haiti, or the Dominican Republic.

The economic history of the "Broken Pledge" period was, in many respects, a showy success story. But by 1930 the twin developments of economic penetration and absentee ownership had been carried to the extreme.

In the field of public utilities and banking the degree of absentee ownership by American corporations was some 60%; in the tobacco industry, 80%; in the sugar industry 60%; in the steamship lines operating between the island ports and mainland ports, almost 100% the latter by reason of the fact that after 1900 the insular economy lost its free bargaining power in that field as a consequence of being placed under the coastwise shipping legislation of the United States, and to the detriment, incidentally, of the island's export costs in comparison with those of her Caribbean neighbors.[16]

. An already bad situation worsened when another destructive hurricane, San Felipe, hit the island in 1928. Storming across the island, it dealt the coffee industry a death blow. Production dropped from 32 million pounds in 1927–28 to 5 million in the following year.[17]

As a result of American colonialism coupled with natural disasters, Puerto Rico by 1930 was on the edge of socioeconomic disaster. Even casual visitors could not help but note the piteous spectacle of poverty and bite-the-fingernail misery of the island people. Malodorous, filthy habitations surrounded the more prosperous areas. Possibly some 35,000 on the island suffered from tuberculosis, some 200,000 from malaria, and some 600,000 from hookworm.[18]

One pitiful story often repeated in the literature of the island tells of a poor family living on the outskirts of the more prosperous metropolitan area. The family secured permission to pick the garbage can of a wealthy upper-class family—to fatten the family sow. Finally the rich family took an interest in the poor family's sow and investigated. But there was no sow on display. There never had been a real sow! The garbage pickings had been used to fill the mouths of growing children.[19]

Part II

The Problem of Puerto Rico

CHAPTER 5

The New Deal and Puerto Rico

AFTER FOUR CENTURIES OF SPANISH COLONIALISM, AS WELL AS three decades under the American brand, Puerto Rico definitely needed reform for its *hombre olvidado* (forgotten man), the *jíbaro*. The miserable conditions which had existed in 1898 were not much better in 1930 despite the honest efforts of those who were working in the areas of general health and education. Hygienic conditions had improved somewhat and this undoubtedly had much to do with the increase in population; in thirty years it had nearly doubled. All the criteria, however, by which a culture is rated, made the island look extremely bad; annual per capita income about $120.00, wages ranging from less than 10¢ to 25¢ per hour, illiteracy still about 70 percent, life expectancy 45 years, and diseases rampant, especially those associated with impure food and water.

Furthermore, Puerto Rico was again subjected to natural disaster. Beginning 10 P.M., September 26, 1932, another severe hurricane, San Cipriano, tore into eastern Puerto Rico and then passed on to the San Juan region and the northwestern coast. This storm did not affect the mountainous coffee zone but the earlier hurricane, San Felipe (1928), had left little there to destroy. Over two hundred persons died and thousands were injured by the damaging winds. The property damage was estimated at 30 million dollars with over 100,000 left homeless. The fact that many of the homes destroyed were mere shacks in El Fanguito (Little Mud), a suburb of San Juan stretching over a stagnant swampy area, did not mitigate, but merely emphasized, the need for economic improvement.

Apparently the situation was not hopeless. In connection with New Deal relief Mrs. Roosevelt visited the island in 1934. To the distress of the members of the American colony, who wished to flaunt the prosperous sites of the wealthy playground, Mrs. Roosevelt took her group across rickety catwalks which exposed the small shacks built from the debris left in the wake of San Cipriano. She and her party saw many poor and jobless dying of malnutrition and tuberculosis. She also visited the hill country where little girls worked at 25¢ an hour, making handerchiefs which sold for a dollar each in New York City. Among the wealth of evidence of hardship she observed a woman carrying a five-gallon water bucket up a steep hillside. Later she found the same woman laboriously scrubbing the floor of her small shack. Despite the misery associated with unemployment and poverty, Mrs. Roosevelt noted that the people possessed self-reliance, self-respect, and a rustic and humble sort of *dignidad*.

As one writer put it succinctly in a pamphlet entitled *Puerto Rico: Fact and Fable,* "What this island needs is a new deal all around with an honest man shuffling the cards."[1] The phrase was prophetic indeed, for shortly would appear two reformers, one an American and the other a Puerto Rican, who would inaugurate changes in both business and politics. But the earlier years of the New Deal period were to be trying indeed for Puerto Ricans.

Ever since the United States took over in 1898 the party affiliation had been influenced by the political status issue or the island's legal relationship to the United States.[2] This situation has continued up to the present. In the election of 1900 the Republican group won on a pro-United States stand. In the next election the Federal Party changed its label to Union and won handily, staying in power for twenty years. This party advocated autonomy for Puerto Rico and represented the upper hacienda-owner class. The Republicans were more pro-United States than the Unionists and also represented influential segments of society, including middle-class businessmen who had connections in New York City and Boston, as well as professionals trained in American universities.

Even before the end of the military government, Puerto Rican leaders began to organize the trade unions. The initiative was taken by Santiago Iglesias, who had been jailed by the Spaniards for similar activities previous to the arrival of the Americans. After gaining his freedom, he organized the Federación Libre de Trabajadores as well as Partido Obrero Socialista. At first, and unsuccessfully, this group made attempts to associate with the Socialist Party in the United States. After several false starts it became the Socialist Party of Puerto Rico. As already noted, it made considerable gains in the elections of the 1920's. By 1932 Santiago Iglesias was considered the dean of liberal Puerto Rican politicans.

In 1922 an extreme group seceded from the Union Party taking the name Nationalists. Because of its slow growth it did not always participate officially in elections, but continued to agitate for complete independence. For the most part this small group was composed of the middle class who looked to Spain for cultural inspiration.

When this group broke away, the *jefe* (chief) of the Unionist Party was Don Antonio Barceló, who assumed leadership when Muñoz Rivera died in 1916. Forming an *Alianza* with some of the Republicans, this group dominated the political scene until the election of 1928, after which the *Alianza* was dissolved. By and large this party promoted little by the way of reform. It kept itself in office by attacking the United States and its representatives. Barceló, for example, was instrumental in the removal of the incompetent Governor E. Mont Reily in 1923.

The two major party groups in the Puerto Rican election of 1932 were the coalition of Union-Republican-Socialists and the Liberal Party. The coalition group was held together by its pro-United States attitude and its fear of the extreme independence element.[3] The newly formed Liberal Party stood for all-out independence and was headed by Barceló who had been pushed out of the Union group. In the election proper the Coalition proved successful, receiving a total of 208,232 votes to 166,235 for the Liberal Party.

The Coalition meeting held at Mayagüez just prior to the election allocated the political plums in the following manner: should the vote be favorable, the Socialists were to name the resident commissioner for Washington, the Union-Republicans the president of the senate, and the party getting the largest vote was to seat the speaker-of-the-house. As a result a humble worker, Santiago Iglesias, would now go to Washington D. C., proving that one from the lowly crowd could scale the heights. On the other hand, although Santiago Iglesias had appreciated the significance of the growth of the Socialist Party and was sympathetic toward American democracy, he still "charged the federal government with neglect because it had allowed Puerto Rico to develop into a sweatshop."[4]

The November election on the continent was a definite victory for one party and apparently for the forgotten man. Could the same be said of the 1932 Puerto Rican election? Not in the opinion of Muñoz Marín who won a senator's seat in that election. This keen observer pointed out that over and above elections, petitions to Congress, the political status issue as well as the home for the new governor—over and above all of these things is the fact that "our people are dying of hunger . . . and in the face of this reality we are playing politics."[5]

Muñoz Marín's comment was specifically aimed at the manner in which the governors were being chosen, but it described politics in general, locally in Puerto Rico and vis-à-vis the United States.

Prospects of a Democratic victory in 1932 had revived the more or less defunct Democratic Party organization in Puerto Rico. Henry W. Dooley, who had been the party leader since Woodrow Wilson's days, died shortly before 1932. This caused a split in the party between the old-line faction whose leaders were the widow of Dooley and the vivacious Jean Whittemore. These leaders backed Benjamin Horton, a lawyer of Mayagüez, for the chairmanship of the group to be seated at the Chicago national convention. Both factions favored Franklin D. Roosevelt for the presidential nomination and differed chiefly on the political status issue. The Horton faction favored statehood whereas the new group controlled by W. Reese Bennett stood for reform of the Jones Act, which would result in more local autonomy as well as an eventual plebiscite on the ultimate status of the island. The Horton group won in a close contest and was accepted by Jim Farley and Governor Roosevelt.

Inasmuch as both groups were composed largely of continentals living in Puerto Rico, their action was not necessarily a true indication of the political trend. Possibly the chief motive for the increased political activity, coupled with intense squabbling, was the hope for the spoils of office. The activities of both groups point up the artificiality of the political activity of the local Democratic Party in the island and the need for reform. Both democratic factions really represented little that was fundamentally Puerto Rican.

The selection of a new governor shows even more clearly the viciousness of the political system, largely on the continental side. Increasingly, sentiment was growing for the appointment of a native Puerto Rican to the office, and there was strong feeling expressed pro and con. James Beverley, the incumbent governor, who had completed one of the best official records previous to 1932, opposed the idea. In his opinion any Puerto Rican appointee would have many family and business connections which might warp his good judgment. Apparently in Puerto Rico, politically speaking, more attention was paid to friendship and kinship than in the United States.

Mrs. James Bourne, a former close neighbor and good friend of the newly elected Franklin Roosevelt and his wife, thought otherwise regarding the governorship. Recently arrived in Puerto Rico to organize a new department in the university, she and her husband kept the Roosevelts informed as to the island's situation. In Dorothy Bourne's opinion, a Puerto Rican "would be *persona grata* to a majority of the Puerto Ricans, if the right person could be found."[6]

Apparently many thought Martin Travieso, a Puerto Rican, the right person and for a time he was seriously considered. The chief marks against him were stressed by the incumbent governor; he was opposed by the party in power, the Coalition group, and he had recently lost heavily in the stock market. Nevertheless, Miss Ruby A. Black gave him a 90 percent chance for the nomination.[7] In addition to his legal career, Travieso had a long and worthy record of political and administrative experience.

Another native with a good record was Dr. José Padín. Padín had served Governor Theodore Roosevelt, Jr., in a cabinet position and as incumbent commissioner of education; he had an excellent record. Both Dorothy Bourne and Governor Beverley, even though the latter had been lukewarm regarding Puerto Ricans, supported him. Lacking press support and organizational backing, he had little chance of being selected, however.

The incumbent himself, James Beverley, might have been the best choice. Having served Governor Roosevelt, Jr., as attorney general he had acquired experience and his own record as governor was one of competence and efficiency. Possibly his service during a Republican administration was his chief handicap. However, he was praised by continentals and Puerto Ricans alike. According to Barceló, Beverley had been criticized and would be in the future: "but we have had no occasion to question the sincerity of his conclusions nor the honesty of his intentions, nor the general worth of his ability."[8]

Apparently such characteristics were not the prime considerations. Even a politically active woman, the lively Jean Whittemore, who had been a delegate to the Democratic National Convention, was mentioned. Typical opposition to her was probably expressed by (another woman), Mrs. Dooley, widow of the deceased party leader, who thought that a woman serving as governor in a Latin country would result in "misery and humiliation" and bring "discredit to our country."

It was something of a surprise and a shock to continentals and Puerto Ricans alike when an unknown, Robert Gore, received the call. A self-made politician noted for generous party contributions, he was favorably recommended and approved by the Senate in May, 1933.

Ruby Black, who had apparently favored Travieso, was "roundly scooped," as were many others. A portent of what was to follow is implied in the description of Miss Black after her interview with the nominee:

He chews gum. He is short, baldish, plump with a dimple. The boys who know him tell me to warn you to nail down the furniture. He seems simple and honest, but if he is, how did he make millions?[9]

Gore knew neither the language of the island nor was he familiar with Spanish culture or character; and he had hoped for "something better." Apparently he didn't know the location of Puerto Rico either, but he aspired to bring the New Deal to that beleaguered isle. As Muñoz Marín had indicated, Puerto Rico in the 1930's was cursed by too much "politics."

The making of a speech at the Century of Progress Fair in Chicago caused a slight delay in Gore's arrival on the island. His speech stressed the necessity of economic revival for Puerto Rico, this in turn depending upon connections with Florida, where he had business interests. Upon his final appearance in Puerto Rico he received the good wishes of everyone. He was welcomed graciously by an editorial in *La Democracia,* the organ of the Liberal Party and Muñoz Marín. But the honeymoon was short. In a month's time Gore made it rather clear that he intended to follow the wishes of the Coalition group rather than those of the Liberals, who were the largest single faction on the island. Moreover, he had ideas of reviving the almost defunct Democratic Party of Puerto Rico. This meant following the wishes of Jim Farley rather than the ideas of the Secretary of War and local leaders.[10] Jean Whittemore, for example, was considered for commissioner of education to replace the competent Dr. José Padín, prompting one critic to observe that "the one activity which has been notably over-developed in Puerto Rico ... is partisan politics."[11] In such an atmosphere conditions grew progressively worse for Gore.

In order to have complete freedom in following his own bent as well as those of continental politicos, Gore made public a request that for the future candidates for public office would be required to submit in advance an undated statement of resignation. This would of course allow greater freedom to himself and Jim Farley. The reaction to this was explosive and the battle broke out into the open. Barceló, for example, immediately withdrew his list of candidates, because he considered such a procedure insulting; he sent a wire to the President of the United States regarding the new governor:

who has so far utterly failed to live up to his early declaration of efficiency and non-politics and has frequently during his short seven weeks grated on the sensibility of our people by uncalled-for grossness of statement culminating in his announcement that he would exact blank resignations from his cabinet.[12]

Encouraged momentarily by support from the Coalition, which represented the pressure groups, the Governor presented a request to the Legislature for remodeling La Fortaleza so that Franklin D. Roosevelt could be wheeled around in proper style. In rather bad taste he also suggested that cockfighting, which many opposed, should be legalized.

On August 21, 1933, the *Washington Daily News* published a cablegram from Gore in which, among other items, he denied that he had required undated resignations from his appointees. He also accused Barceló of not cooperating and of being an "old man who has about lost his power and is crying in the wilderness." Later, while visiting Washington, D.C., Gore was personally handed an editorial from *La Democracia* entitled "Governor Gore, you are a Damn Liar." The final paragraph indicated that the accusation had been made deliberately so the Governor could sue for libel if he had not lied. "It is in your hand to demonstrate your veracity."[13]

This type of politics absorbed the energy of Puerto Rican

politicos and of the Governor while serious legislation failed to materialize. In addition to the request for undated resignations, Gore's attempt to unseat Dr. José Padín as Commissioner of Education was extremely unwise and proved to be the main cause for his downfall. Gore opposed Padín because, in his opinion, the schools of Puerto Rico were not pro-American, English was taught with "left-handed gestures," and the minds of students were instilled with the ultimate idea of independence. Padín's record, however, was excellent. He had been one of a select group of young Puerto Rican students picked by the United States Government in 1900 to be educated on the mainland. He eventually secured a doctor's degree from Columbia University. When called back to the island, he left a high-paying position with D. C. Heath and Co. During Theodore Roosevelt, Jr.'s, term as governor in Puerto Rico, he had served well and was considered apolitical. He was opposed by the ultra 100 percent-Americans who wished to discard entirely the Spanish heritage. Probably the basic charge against Padín was that he served as an educator, not a politician. To him the making of good Puerto Ricans was the same as creating good Americans. In this controversy Padín was backed by the common people as well as by knowledgeable Puerto Ricans and continentals. The following quote comes from the private correspondence of a Puerto Rican woman, who pointed out that Gore was hated and scorned because he was a sap, "drank like a lord," promoted cock fights and demanded blank-advance resignations of public officials. Puerto Ricans wanted him "kicked out."[14]

The opinion of Dr. Leland Jenks of Wellesley College is typical of the continentals who supported Padín, including former Governor Beverley and Dr. Ernest Hopkins of Dartmouth. Such observers had the highest respect for his abilities and felt that he had assimilated the best that United States had to offer in the field of modern educational policies, applicable to Puerto Rican schools.[15]

A further indication that Gore was playing politics in his appointments is clearly shown by his naming of Rafael Alonzo

Torres to the University Board of Directors. Alonzo Torres was a Socialist member of the House. The requirements called for a man of "science, letters and arts" and Torres was a self-made politician who had little formal education.

As a result of these machinations, Gore became the object of Puerto Rican satire. The island wags worked out a farce entitled "Gore's Hell." The main characters were Don Antonio de la Mancha (Barceló), Gorito Dantes (Gore), Tio Samuel (Uncle Sam), María del Mar (Puerto Rico), and her suitor Benjamin (independence). The plot centered around Gorito Dantes who considered himself sent by the Celestial Father, Gran Delanito, to win María del Mar. In this he failed because he demanded unsigned divorce papers. Apparently the play was an enormous success on the island; the Coalition even took steps to prevent its showing in Mayagüez.

Although Franklin D. Roosevelt had made a mistake in the beginning, he and his wife were getting the island's story from people such as James and Dorothy Bourne, Muñoz Marín, and Ruby Black. Inasmuch as Gore was making the Padín controversy a personal "either him or me proposition," the President decided to agree with Dr. Ernest Hopkins who in a memorandum to Secretary of War Dern stated, "He is probably the worst blunderer that ever came along.... He has a genius for doing things wrong and has a feeling of hostility or suspicion toward anybody not connected with [his] political group...."[16]

On October 24, 1933, La Democracia carried a profound editorial on the role of executive responsibility in the Puerto Rican government; it stressed the need of the Puerto Ricans for pride in their race, language, and future:

And we may add, it is essential in the prestige of the United States, in the eyes of the Latin American peoples, that no slightest shadow of suspicion shall be cast that the United States is consciously playing politics with the will of the Puerto Rican people, with their struggle to define their own future themselves.[17]

Apparently Franklin D. Roosevelt thought similarly because on January 12, 1934, he accepted Governor Gore's resignation;

thus María del Mar had been relieved of an unwanted lover by El Gran Delanito.

Gore's administration provided the tone for the "reforming" 1930's and also indicated how paradoxical the situation was. Some New Deal appointees attempting "reform" really didn't understand what was needed. Puerto Rico was ripe for real revolutionary change—with honest men carrying the banner. The mote in the eye of the affluent, dominant countries has not always been evil intent, but rather, a profound lack of understanding coupled with a smug certainty that often characterizes those who possess wealth and power. The governors who followed Gore in the 1930's could not help but be an improvement, but basically conditions changed little.

After the terrible hurricane of 1928 much aid had been allotted to Puerto Rico; 4.1 million in direct relief and 6 million in loans to agriculturists. During the transition period of the New Deal another million or so was lent by the Reconstruction Finance Corporation for economic assistance. Through December, 1938, the PRRA (Puerto Rican Reconstruction Administration) had granted $57,953,189.24 on various phases of its program.[18] Efforts had been made to extend the most important aspects of the New Deal to the island, but before the real benefits could reach the lower classes the programs had usually been emasculated by the courts or the corrupt political situation. This tendency is well illustrated by the action of the two parties as regards workmen's compensation during Governor Beverley's administration. Because Union Republicans as well as Socialists seemed to be more concerned with the attitude of the business interests than with the workers, the conservative but honest governor pointed out that the principal question was not the expense of the system but the terrible fact that—in spite of heavy expense—injured laborers were receiving no benefits. In his opinion the object of workmen's compensation laws was to protect the laborer and not to protect and benefit politicians, lawyers, and doctors.[19] The curious establishment which had grown up as a result of the Jones Act resulted in a political situation where no one was responsible to the woman doing needlework for 25c an hour, or to the *jíbaro* recently moved to El Fanguito.

There was the Chardón Plan, for example. Undoubtedly it was the brainchild of Rexford Guy Tugwell as a result of his tour of the island in 1934. It called for the socialization of the sugar industry, the establishment of many light domestic industries (rum, bottles, cellulose), growing of vegetables as a communal affair, and the promotion of birth control.[20]

This plan got its name from the chancellor of the University, Carlos Chardón, and had his support as well as that of other liberals. It died aborning due to the confused political situation.

Even though men with extremely liberal ideals were appointed to serve during this period, important changes did not take place. Another conspicuous leader of this type was Dr. Ernest Gruening, whose record was almost spotlessly perfect. He had been editor of *The Nation* and had written a book on *Mexico and Its Heritage* and was considered, and considered himself, to be an expert on Latin American affairs, especially the Caribbean region. In 1934 he was appointed to the headship of DTIP (Division of Territories and Island Possessions), and later served as P.R.R.A. administrator. As editor of *The Nation,* Gruening had befriended Muñoz Marín by publishing his writings and when appointed to head the DTIP one well-known liberal commented, "Not in all the years that I have been writing ... can I recall an appointment which has given ... more satisfaction."[21]

Nevertheless, Gruening ended up by feuding with Muñoz Marín and displaying an uncompromising attitude toward those who disagreed with him. Moreover, Gruening was also responsible for the failure of many New Deal measures in Puerto Rico. Unfortunately he and some of those he criticized were not responsive politically to the same people.

The election of 1936 offered some hope. It appeared that the Liberal Party, guided by men like Muñoz Marín, was headed for certain victory. Moreover, the New Deal was beginning to function and it looked as though Puerto Ricans would always have a sufficient supply of *bacalao* and *arroz* (fish and rice). A series of events spoiled all this, however, principally the assassination of Colonel Francis Riggs, chief of insular police, on February 23, 1936, the police reprisals which followed, and Nationalist reaction for complete independence. As a result of the riots and killings, eight Nationalists were tried on July 14, 1936; they were found guilty by a jury of ten residential continentals and only two Puerto Ricans in a country where lived several millions of them. The eight were sentenced to the Atlanta Federal Prison for a period of from two to ten years. But the applause which accompanied these prisoners as they strode from the trial to the island prison was similar to that accorded the seven bishops who disagreed with James II in the England of 1689. It was a portent of trouble for Puerto Rican politics, as the Ponce "massacre" indicates.[22]

While all this turbulence transpired, the United States Senate was considering the Tydings Bill which would give Puerto Rico a chance to vote on independence; this tended to "widen and deepen" the influence of the extreme Nationalists. It also split the Liberal Party. Muñoz Marín, who had led the early independence movement, was not in favor of independence without guarantees for Puerto Rican welfare, through such means as proper trade quotas and incentives to manufacturers. As a result, he angered the extremists, and the *politicos* read him out of the party. But, by this time Muñoz was pretty much the Liberal Party. As one paper, *Florete,* put it, "Barceló kicks out the Liberal Party." Muñoz Marín would have to wait for another day—or possibly for a revolution.

In 1936, as in 1900 and 1930, Puerto Rico was a lovely spot for the tourist—especially because of the water, the mountains, and tropical vegetation. In the mountains, however, the *jíbaro* had little money, little education, very little electricity or safe drinking water.

Although the island was a ward of the wealthiest of nations, its annual per capita income was still only $121.00, and wages in the sugar-cane industry were 14c an hour. In 1942 a minister from Mayagüez wrote Eleanor Roosevelt regarding conditions of the school children slowly starving: ... "because when they live at a distance, and have not even had a cup of black coffee for breakfast or lunch, they are just too weak to come. One girl did come one day, and fell over on the cement floor, she was so weak, without anything to eat."[23]

As Muñoz Marín stated, "In Puerto Rico we do not have a submerged third, but we do have a floating and sometimes drowning 90%—and a buoyant 10%."[24]

After four centuries of Spanish and four decades of American colonialism, Puerto Rico needed change, a revolutionary change that would bring identity to her people, individual and collective. Puerto Rico in 1940 faced twentieth-century problems with obsolete eighteenth-century machinery.

CHAPTER 6

Reformers

INASMUCH AS PUERTO RICO HAD BEEN EXPOSED TO MULTIRACIAL as well as multinational influences, it is not surprising that its first real reform came as a result of men representing different cultural backgrounds: Luis Muñoz Marín, the Puerto Rican-Iberian, and Rexford Guy Tugwell, the Anglo-American. The success of the reform movement owes much to both men. Moreover, it is not unnatural that the basic work or reform of Muñoz Marín should precede that of Tugwell because any real reform must be largely the work of the people benefiting from the changes. The quiet revolution was not and is not without problems; its original rallying cry was "Manos a la obra" (Let's get on with the job) and Muñoz Marín was responsible for the seminal reforms at the outset.

It would almost appear that Muñoz Marín was destined to lead Puerto Rico as a revolutionary statesman. He was born in San Juan, near Fortaleza, in 1898. As we have indicated, his father, Luis Muñoz Rivera, a crusading statesman at the turn of the century, had achieved autonomy for Puerto Rico by the Sagasta Pact of 1897. His father was also editor of the liberal newspaper, *La Democracia*, and had founded the long dominant Union Party.

Muñoz Marín's youth was such that he became a product of two cultures. His early education was achieved on the island and in New York City. Later he studied journalism at Columbia University and law at Georgetown University. He wrote, thought, and spoke fluently both Spanish and English. He contributed to the *American Mercury, Nation*, and the *New Republic*. He had translated the poem of Edwin Markham's (whom he knew and admired), "The Man With a Hoe," into Spanish.

[65]

Muñoz Marín developed into a combination of the traditional Latin-American poet-intellectual-statesman, and the American-style politician. He possessed the savoir-faire of the former and the *realpolitik* of the latter. As a young intellectual he probably found it difficult to accept the backwardness associated with his Spanish background, the Puerto Rican tendency toward political reaction as well as shortcomings in science and technology. The progressivism of the United States he accepted. In fact, he campaigned for Robert M. LaFollette in the 1924 presidential election. He had become acquainted with the practical aspects of American politics, and he needed this knowledge to understand the machinations of the "New Deal" in Puerto Rico. In Tugwell's book *The Art of Politics; As Practiced by Three Great Americans: Franklin D. Roosevelt, Luis Muñoz Marín, and Fiorello H. LaGuardia,*[1] the author praises Muñoz Marín very highly. As a *patrón* and native *hombre del pueblo,* (man of the people) he was a *criollo* (Spaniard born in West Indies) and Puerto Rican, but in his political pragmatism he was a *yanqui* (American). The combination is what Puerto Rico seemed to need after the election of 1936.

The Puerto Rican Reconstruction Administration and New Deal efforts had pretty much failed in Puerto Rico. The reason was largely due to the curious and vicious political system which had grown up as a result of American colonialism under the Jones Act.

Despite the note of despair after 1936, however, all did not seem to be lost. The laissez-faire attitude of the United States Government had been more or less reversed. Apparently four decades of colonial neglect and exploitation were to be undone by research, investigation, planning, and regulation. There was, however, danger also in too much regulation from the outside. It is exactly here where Muñoz Marín played such an important role when he pointed out that his people had suffered from a lack of political power as well as lack of sufficient natural resources: "But it is also true that we have never in our history, consciously and with determination, set out to do the very best we can with the powers and resources we do have. Let us try that and see what happens."[2]

Did this mean that Puerto Rico had to work for independence, or could economic justice and progress be achieved under the old order, somewhat modified?

The hard-core independence movement had gained support due to the lagging New Deal efforts as well as the "witch hunting" practices of Dr. Gruening. Muñoz Marín himself had been one of the spokesmen for the *independentistas* and had written the plank for the Liberal Party on this issue. Very early, however, he realized that unconditional independence could work to the disadvantage of the island's main economic activity, the growing of sugar, as well as other produce. As early as 1932, he pointed out in *La Democracia* that sugar production in Puerto Rico would have been impossible without the protection of the United States tariff under which it operated. What Puerto Rico needed, he felt, was economic reform and social justice, which could, possibly, best be achieved under some form of meaningful autonomy. In 1934 Muñoz Marín stated that: "The issue . . . lies between statehood on the one hand, and independence or autonomy on the other."[3] Expanding this concept of independence also broadened his support, because the shibboleth of independence had strong emotional appeal.

Friction over the Tydings Bill, the Riggs assassination, and the consequent repercussions made it extremely difficult for Muñoz Marín to take a clear-cut stand on the independence issue. Increasingly he began to see that it was more important to work for political reform and economic justice than to satisfy the extremists on independence. Seeing the Liberal Party hopelessly split before the election of 1936, he decided to resign as its leader. Many saw this as a mistake on his part—*un retraimiento* (retreat). Even his friends in Washington took this attitude, fearing that he might lose his entrée in the capital. Muñoz Marín realized that his action was like that of Cortés at Vera Cruz when he burned his ships, making it impossible to turn back. That Muñoz Marín appreciated the gravity of the situation is clear from his 1936 comment. He realized that a goodly number of the party—possibly one third—were opposed to his decision, but:

> If I split the party, I shall have these people against me for the next 30 years. If I preserve the solidarity of the party on my own volition, and even against the proven wishes of the other group, I shall have all these people with me forever . . .[4]

The Liberal Party did split and die with the 1936 election, but the success of the new party, Populares, in the 1940 election proved that Muñoz Marín sank the right ships!

Fraud had characterized past elections in Puerto Rican history. Efforts had been made, however, to bring about reform and some progress was forthcoming. As long as the *jíbaro* continued to sell his vote, however, such reforms were meaningless.

The campaign which Muñoz Marín launched and carried out (1938–40) was much like that of Lázaro Cárdenas in Mexico in 1934 when the latter stumped the country, appealing to the *campesino*. With the slogan, "Bread, land and liberty" (much like the Mexican Emiliano Zapata's *Tierra y libertad*), Muñoz Marín crisscrossed the country, soliciting support from "The sometimes drowning 90%." His emblem was the pava, the *jíbaro* hat. Capitalizing on his writing ability, he utilized his own paper *La Democracia* as well as a free campaign newspaper, *El Batey*.[5]

The specifics of the campaign and election of 1940 are withal so significant that they merit special treatment and labeling. *Jalda Arriba!* (Up the hill!) characterized the struggle and became one of its slogans. The whole affair was a drama of Shakespearean proportions.

To appreciate fully the nature of the task it must be remembered that Puerto Rico had "enjoyed" a Socialist Party since the turn of the century and the political goal of men like Santiago Iglesias for a long time had been the good and decent life. Muñoz had to be "tireless, lucid, and finally persuasive" to believe that the *jíbaro*, who was often on the verge of starvation, should refuse to sell his vote for $2.00.

Muñoz had no organizational support at first. At the outset of the campaign, *La Democracia* was defunct, and *El Vate* (The bard) himself had little or no money to go on the air. Nevertheless, his humor and wit reached the people. He needed a car and driver, for example, "who could make a car move without gasoline, who could live without food and who could work for pennies a day."[6] He realized that $2.00 meant immediate satisfaction in terms of beans, rice, and fish, but he apparently convinced the *jíbaro* that he couldn't have that and social justice also. Furthermore, this election again deemphasized the status issue: "The Popular Party wants to say that it has a solemn obligation to the people not to interpret the votes cast in favor of the . . . party as votes in favor of any particular status."[7]

In his efforts to reach the *jíbaro* as well as other classes, Muñoz personally canvassed 500 of the 786 electoral districts. Moreover, *El Batey* (the campaign newspaper), was becoming successful and not a financial burden; even members of the opposition felt themselves compelled to use it for advertising.

Many had considered Muñoz's political career ended after the unfortunate events related to the 1936 election. At first sarcastic remarks from opposition groups appeared in the newspapers labeling the *El Batey* gatherings as boys' club meetings of anti-American Communists. Muñoz, however, directed his appeal to all classes—the *jíbaro* as well as other groups because he felt the misery of the people had wrought a condition of extreme desperation: "I speak to the working class, I speak to the agricultural class, I speak, because only with justice done with order and in time will chaos be avoided . . ."[8]

Gradually his campaign came to embrace a whole cross section of society—cane cutters, teachers, dock workers, Negroes, and Hispanic whites. Moreover, Muñoz Marín apparently convinced the *jíbaro* that selling his vote was like throwing away a machete in the midst of a fight. The 1938–40 campaign was unique in that it was not based on hatred or violence. One keen observer emphasized that a worthwhile leader should not capitalize on hatred and violence but should have a more significant frame of reference: "He won't be representing any group such as the Negroes or the Catholics or the sugar interests. Instead, he'll regard the entire interests of the island, and he should go farther than that and think in terms of a world society."[9]

Moreover, Muñoz began to appear as a patriot to all, even to some of those who formed the opposition. Several times his driver had difficulty buying gas because of party feelings. On one such occasion, his driver roused the only service station owner who happened to be a staunch Republican. "I will vote against him a hundred times if I can" said this proprietor—"but he is our greatest patriot—let's fill his tank."[10]

Probably Muñoz's greatest thrill during the campaign was the candlelight audience—one late evening. Fearing Muñoz's growing influence, hacienda owners began forbidding *jíbaro* attendance at his gatherings. On this occasion he set up a loudspeaker on a rather lonely mountain road overlooking a valley. There were only a few present and obviously he needed no loudspeaker for them. But one in the audience pointed to the microphone and smiled, "Go ahead, talk. Talk loud." Soon tiny lights appeared in the blanket of darkness. Questioningly Muñoz looked at his grinning peasant audience. "They light their candles," it was explained "to let you know they can hear."[11]

But Muñoz still had a nagging worry. How could he be sure that come voting time the $2.00 would not be more potent than promises. On September 15, 1940, therefore, Muñoz held a Popular Party rally on a streetcorner of Santurce. Before a crowd of some 15,000, the party leaders swore publicly to vote for and to uphold the promised reform program.

Finally the vote came in and all the campaign efforts were vindicated. Muñoz and some of his close associates awaited electoral returns at the home of an old friend. With the coffee hot and the radio playing, the result came over the air. Bayamón, a formerly staunch Republican district, reported a modest Coalition (Republican and Socialist) showing and a strong registration for the *Populares*. Muñoz, in the attitude of a college cheerleader, exploded: "They are doing it! They are doing it! They have refused to sell their votes! . . . Those wonderful people. They are starving and they haven't let me down."[12]

The election was not a landslide, but by winning ten of the eighteen senatorial seats, Muñoz, who received the largest vote of the candidates for senator at large, was able to dominate the political situation and bring on real reform. This in turn led to landslides later.[13]

Apparently some aspects of politics were distasteful to Muñoz. Nearly exhausted from the campaign, he fled to the home of a friend, Elmer Ellsworth, for recuperation. No one was to be granted an audience except members of his family and any *jíbaro* who might call. According to Earl Parker Hanson, an aged *campesino* had sold two of his chickens so he could travel to Muñoz and there kneel and pray—this he had promised the Virgin. "A man must keep his promises," said Muñoz and he saw no reason why he shouldn't kneel also. Inasmuch as the aged man had sold his chickens for the trip, friends suggested that Muñoz pay for a round trip. Muñoz's answer was "When a man offers you his soul do you give him small change?"[14] The *jíbaro* was returned home in Muñoz's own car.

Three weeks after the 1940 elections Muñoz Marín wrote to Franklin D. Roosevelt and pledged his cooperation. He concluded the message with a request: "Help us, Mr. President, so that the democracy discovered in . . . our unhappy people may be of the fullest use to themselves."[15]

The President complied by sending Rexford Guy Tugwell to that stricken land. If destiny had picked Muñoz Marín to inaugurate revolutionary change in Puerto Rico, surely *El Gran Delanito* (Celestial Father) had cooperated fully by sending a true liberal to be a collaborator.

Born in Sinclairville, New York, in 1891, Tugwell grew up in the small-town atmosphere of that state. High school education was obtained at Buffalo and advanced degrees in economics at the Wharton School of the University of Pennsylvania. Since he was ambitious, and, like Muñoz Marín, a poet, Tugwell's early life is marked by teaching, writing, and much concern with governmental planning, Along with other liberals, Tugwell had concluded that dangers associated with the growing power of big business, big labor, and technology, had caused or would cause the demise of nineteenth-century laissez-faire. Progress would be achieved by cooperative planning between government and business. Tugwell made it clear in his writings, however, that all totalitarian, doctrinaire solutions, including the Marxian, should be rejected.[16] Nevertheless, it is axiomatic that new ideas frighten the old order and are usually labeled accordingly. It is not surprising, therefore, that Tugwell as Under Secretary of the Department of Agriculture (1933–37) and chairman of the New York Planning Commission (1938) was one of the most controversial of the New Dealers. Because of their literary abilities and liberal ideas both Muñoz Marín and Tugwell were viewed in curious contradiction as "dreamers," and yet "dangerous revolutionaries."

While being investigated by the United States Senate for the job of governor of Puerto Rico, Tugwell also considered the position of Chancellor of the University of Puerto Rico.[17] On the way to San Juan to give the University's opening address, he read in the *Miami Herald* critical remarks made by Senator Taft, who opposed his nomination for the office of governor. Taft denounced the whole New Deal as socialistic and accepted the newspaper stereotype of Tugwell as "the worst administrator who ever lived, and a failure at everything he ever tried."[18]

Despite such opposition, Tugwell's appointment was confirmed by the United States Senate and on September 19, 1941, he took the oath of office as governor of Puerto Rico.

As a representative of the Department of Agriculture, Tugwell had toured Puerto Rico in the 1930's and was acquainted with its problems as well as its political shortcomings.

Franklin D. Roosevelt was also aware of the exploitation of the island. Before Tugwell's 1941 departure, Roosevelt wanted to know whether the slums were gone and if there was safe drinking water on the island. Tugwell was not long in finding that conditions had improved little since his earlier visits. The shack city of squatters' houses called El Fanguito was characterized by him as a "homunculus or some other low form of life" which had "a kind of order and governance of its own."

It had been Governor Winship's (1934–39) ambition to secure pure water for San Juan, and Tugwell's first question at his hotel raised that point. The immediate answer was "Hell, the water's filthy and most of the time it's shut off." This was later confirmed by the desk attendant who informed Tugwell that all guest water was boiled. Later, after a walk in the hot streets, he found that the hotel "shower bath" refused to function. The response to complaints regarding such conditions was often "*Ah bendito*" (Oh blessed).[19]

However, the "*Ah bendito*" syndrome did not characterize the thinking of the two reformers, Muñoz Marín and Tugwell. The final line of one of Tugwell's poems ended, "I shall roll up my sleeves—make America over." Apparently the elite who had enjoyed the status quo had reason to be concerned. The Puerto Rican situation was complex and demanded cooperation between the appointed executive and the locus of political power.

Tugwell, a pragmatist, could see that the Puerto Rican legislature had successfully emasculated the power of the appointed governor. In his words, "Puerto Rican ingenuity had defeated the United States occupation." But Tugwell also realized that progress would not result if all appointments were the results of narrow political interests. According to the Jones Act of 1917, administrative appointments were subject to Senate (Puerto Rican) approval. Gradually a policy called the *terna* (three) had developed. Three of the most important advisers to the governor (the Commissioner of Education, the Attorney General, and the Auditor) were, according to the organic law, to be appointed by the executive himself. However, the *terna* was a list of candidates submitted to the governor by the leader of the Puerto Rican legislature. Appointees so named obviously

owed loyalty to Puerto Rican leaders and not to the governor. It had become the policy of the Senate not to approve
candidates other than those included in the *terna*. The legislature even went beyond the constitutional requirements of the
Jones Act and stipulated by law that lesser officials also be subject to legislative confirmation. The situation called for understanding and cooperation.

Shortly after Tugwell assumed office, Muñoz Marín agreed to
eliminate the *terna*. This came after friction had developed over
two rather important appointments. Informal consultation and
compromise replaced the dictatorial policy of the past. Muñoz
did not insist on naming every appointee, and Tugwell often
suggested individuals he considered qualified. It is significant,
however, that most of Tugwell's early appointments were *Populares* and not Coalitionists. Inasmuch as both reformers were
intellectual pragmatists and ardent liberals in the New Deal
sense, it would appear that the old sterile rivalry between *La
Fortaleza* (the governor's mansion) and *El Capitolio* (the legislative power) would be replaced by enlightened cooperation.
This situation meant that self-participatory democracy was being
achieved, and rare indeed are the instances when such change
occurs without war, violence, and/or destruction. The philos-
ophies and abilities of both reformers were needed.

The social and economic problems which had plagued Puerto
Rico were obvious and they were legion. It was also clear to
the reformers that new personnel was essential. The character of
the new men as well as the nature of the reforms are illustrated
by the manner in which Guillermo Nigaglioni was discovered
by Tugwell. One day in 1942 Tugwell's aide took the governor's
tax report to Nigaglioni's office for filing. Nigaglioni refused to
accept the return because the report had not been notarized.
This procedure shocked the aide, but not Tugwell, who as a
result promptly hired the young man as Assistant Director of
the Budget.

Many of the new men were of this type; conscientious, young,
educated, and honest. Roberto Sanchez Vilella, a tall, hand-

some engineer who had attended Ohio State University, took over the Puerto Rican Transportation Authority. Another was Rafael Pico, a Ph.D. from Clark University, who became the first chairman of the Puerto Rican Planning Board. Jaime Benítez, with a master's degree from Georgetown, was appointed Chancellor of the University of Puerto Rico. Antonio Fernós-Isern, an M.D. from the University of Maryland and a man of reputation in health circles on the island, became Commissioner of Health. There were others.

Teodoro Moscoso illustrates well the bi-cultural nature of the reforms taking place in Puerto Rico as well as the kind of leadership needed. He had attended the Philadelphia College of Pharmacy and Science and the University of Michigan. He was successfully engaged in the drug business in the city of Ponce when Muñoz and Tugwell agreed that he was the man needed to run the key Industrial Development Company of Operation Bootstrap. Here he achieved fame; also later as director of the Alliance for Progress.

Moscoso was a dedicated, hard-driving, impressive young man who apparently possessed "animal energy." This master administrator became the pivot of the island's new economic machine. Apparently he shared the knowledge and urgency of the situation common to both Tugwell and Muñoz. In his office headquarters a sign read: "Please be brief. We are already twenty-five years late."[20]

Obviously these were not appointments based on party politics. In fact, these bright, young Puerto Ricans were a bit scornful of the political crowd, and years later one of them stated that Muñoz himself "didn't know a planning board from a parole board." With this talent around him, Muñoz was forced to take a refresher course in economics.

In all areas demanding reform, research was necessary. The nature of the problem is illustrated by the transportation system of the island about which little was known then. One of the basic tasks was given to the Mapping Division of the Planning Board. As a result a long-range plan was worked out for rural Puerto

Rico as well as for San Juan. But there was opposition. At a public hearing on the problem some questioned the reasonableness of such a colossal enterprise for a city of less than 250,000. Today every driver in congested San Juan (with approximately a half million people) should realize the need for enlightened planning.

This was, of course, Tugwell's forte and he had worked for a planning board independent of the executive as well as of political pressure of partisan politics in the legislature—in other words a sort of "fourth power." The bill which created the Puerto Rican Planning Board in 1942 was somewhat modified by the legislature. Tugwell got essentially what he wanted, however, largely due to the cooperation of Muñoz.

We were adopting a whole new program for Puerto Rico; he came to regard the Bureau of the Budget and the Planning Board as necessary instruments, along with others, of that program. And he saw to it that the enabling act was passed, even if not exactly as we wanted it.[21]

But the session of April, 1942, was controversial and heated indeed. It ran overtime and clocks were stopped. Members were exhausted and some went to the hospital. Because his margin of control was so slim, Muñoz had some legislators hauled back on stretchers to vote. The bill passed, and it provided for planning and reform in almost all essential areas, such as the water system, the fire service, the transportation and communication systems, and the sugar industry.

Tugwell's great contribution was his knowledge of planning and administration. He really taught the political leaders how to run a governmental machine and this helped promote desirable reforms. Even his bitterest enemies have not been able to negate or nullify this achievement.

As indicated, opposition was strong and vocal, but there was progress. The Land Authority's work included supervision and control of some 110,000 acres of sugar-cane land. This Authority had been empowered to purchase, for just compensation, land held by private individuals or corporations in excess of 500 acres. To the extent feasible, sugar mills remained in private hands. Sugar production, to be profitable, must be a large-scale operation, and this caused some private entrepreneurs to be put back on the land. All in all, the government was to employ 20 percent of the sugar workers, own two sugar mills, and establish 143 rural villages by resettling 17,631 subsistence-farmer families. Criticism would naturally arise from the concerned interests in both the continental United States and Puerto Rico. Tugwell acquired the nickname "Rex the Red" for his "half-baked socialistic program."

Probably the most bitter criticism resulted from the reform of the most glaring of evils—partisan politics and the undrinkable water of San Juan. As a result of the planning and reform program, the unreliable municipal water systems were transferred to the Water Resources Authority. Although the Popular Party gained control of the Senate in the election of 1940, the Coalition Party had more votes and, as a result Bolivar Pagán became Resident Commissioner in Washington. Much of his support came from his control of the water system in San Juan. He criticized and demanded the resignation of Tugwell because—in his opinion —the island was on the verge of revolution. He called for the enforcement of the Organic Act and the ousting of Tugwell in order to reestablish in Puerto Rico the government of law and order. "Tugwell's dictatorial attitude can be matched only by Hitler's and Mussolini's tactics. . . . We have a most scandalous situation. . . . Puerto Rico is overexcited and almost on the verge of revolution."[22]

Despite the need for patriotic, loyal cooperation during the war period, Tugwell was criticized severely by the newspapers in Puerto Rico and the United States. In 1943 several insular affairs committees as well as two Congressional committees (one Senate Committee headed by Dennis Chavez of New Mexico and another House Committee chaired by C. Jasper Bell of Missouri) came to see what Tugwell was "up to down there." The opposition was so strong that funds Tugwell had expected to use for the production of food instead of sugar were withheld by the House Agricultural Committee. While Tugwell was governor, Senator Vandenberg even introduced a bill to terminate the office of governor for Puerto Rico and thereby accomplish legislative removal.[23]

Although critics and opposition groups succeeded in causing temporary and serious setbacks for the Puerto Rican revolution, especially during the World War II period, ultimately they failed. The reform laws remained in force and Tugwell remained in office. With staunch support from President Franklin D. Roosevelt, Secretary Ickes, and Muñoz Marín, Tugwell continued as governor long after the criticism had died down.

The election results in 1944 must have been a great source of joy to both Tugwell and Muñoz Marín. The theme stressed by Muñoz in this campaign was that the *Populares* had kept their promises, but they might have done more with full political control. Apparently the people accepted this thesis. The *Populares* got 383,280 votes against 101,779 for the Union Republicans, the second contending party. In the previous Senate the *Populares* had a majority of only one; now it was 17 to 2. In the House, where the Tripartite Party had held the balance with three members after the 1940 election, the count was now: *Populares* 37, the opposition 2! Moreover, the conservative Resident Commissioner, Bolívar Pagán, was replaced by Jesús Piñero. Joyous wags spread the story of the significant victory by claiming that the *Populares* had caused "Jesús to replace the Pagán" in Washington.

Moreover, it was a victory for Tugwell, as well as for Muñoz Marín and his party. The victory was so overwhelming that even the most rabid and contentious *Coalicionista* could not explain away the defeat. It was magnificent for the victors and ignominious for the losers. Obviously, Tugwell had not participated personally in the campaign, but his reputation was very much involved. He had been praised by the victors and vilified by the losers. If the electoral results were a victory for enlightened government, then his behavior had been correct. Apparently he felt the time appropriate for "celebration . . . with my friends."

Undoubtedly the top leadership in Puerto Rican politics since 1940 had been exceedingly creative. Muñoz Marín had taught the people how to build a truly democratic, popularly based party. Furthermore, he had shifted attention from the political status issue to economic and social justice.

As Muñoz was creative in politics, Tugwell was creative in planning and the administration of planning, although his expertise was unappreciated by die-hard conservatives.

Both Muñoz Marín and Tugwell were young, liberal intellectuals. Both were poets. It might be said that "the poets in the fortress," had, for a time, bested Sisyphus,[24] and in so doing laid the basis for further significant reforms.

CHAPTER 7

Reforms

AFTER HIS SIGNIFICANT VICTORY AT THE POLLS IN 1944, MUÑOZ wrote a series of carefully prepared articles and essays for *El Mundo*, Puerto Rico's leading newspaper at that time. Herein he expressed ideas regarding the political status issue and liberty. In "New Solutions for Old Problems" he stated: "We have been arguing traffic rules for victorias and buggies in a time of automobiles and airplanes." Pointing to the need for new thinking for tribal nations in a world of nuclear power he argued: "If sovereignty is one form of liberty and freeing oneself from the threat of war is another form of liberty, humanity must choose which of the two forms it prefers, because one is clearly incompatible with the other." He was laying the basis for his commonwealth stand as well as further internal social and juridical reforms. In his opinion, Puerto Rico could achieve self-government without slavery under whatever political status:

... If liberty from the fear of hunger is one liberty, and the freedom to govern oneself without the economic means to eliminate the fear of hunger is another liberty, then we must find how to avoid that one such liberty should destroy the other ...[1]

Demands which arise from the pit of the stomach were apparently the first concern of Muñoz Marín. As a result a program of social rehabilitation and economic reconstruction acquired fame under the name "Operation Bootstrap." Actually, this program had been launched after the Popular Party victory at the polls in 1940, but the nickname came later. As indicated above, social and economic change was promoted on a broad front preceded by governmental research and planning. No less than fourteen public or semipublic corporations were established to bring about economic and social progress on interlocking fronts.

By the time Muñoz was ready to run for governor (1948), he could lay claim to reforms in the sugar industry, housing, medical aid, educational facilities, rural electrification, physical fitness programs, better highways, and special aid for indigents and the aged. During that period, for example, sugar workers had been employed and were earning some 5 million dollars—half a million in profit sharing. Almost 200,000 school children were receiving free lunches. Over 90,000 former *jíbaro* tenants now lived in their own houses on their own plots of land. Collectively, the government corporations represented a substantial portion of the insular work force, about 17 percent in 1945.[2] With the exception of the Water Resources Authority, the Aqueduct and Sewer Service, the Transportation Authority, and the Development Bank, government corporations were economic failures. The intangible benefits, however, measured in terms of general welfare and the promotion of a more utilitarian philosophy would seem to justify labeling the program a success. Naturally there was criticism from the conservative forces in the United States and Puerto Rico. One United States Congressman, for example, lamented the fact that while the nation as a whole was moving toward sensible postwar reconversion, almost every conceivable phase of life and activity in Puerto Rico was subject to "obligatory socialism." Even Teodoro Moscoso, who headed *Fomento*[3] and was general manager of the program after 1942, in a letter to Auditor Cordero criticized as follows:

Apparently government-in-competitive-business simply does not work in a democracy; the morale of managers, supervisory personnel and even labor is extremely hard to maintain in an industrial enterprise created within a political framework. Copies of your Public Corporation Audit Division's reports go to all our managers and invariably the result is a considerable reduction in the initiative and willingness to take normal business risks. They begin to think in terms of covering themselves, of keeping their records clean rather than in terms of making a success out of their business in competition with competitors who are not tied down by the fetters of government bureaucracy.[4]

Muñoz and his colleagues had decided by 1947 to seek support for the industrial program from private business and to have government funds aid individual firms. By contrast with the service activities[5] of the *Fomento* program, all the manufacturing enterprises of the government were failures except one, the Cement Corporation. After 1942, under the direction of the Developmental Company, five government-built plants endeavored to make glass bottles and paper cardboard for the rum industry, clay products, shoes, leather goods, and cement. The cement company was a great success, but the others lost money due to incompetence. Moreover, as the war came to a close, the rum boom and the raison d'être for the glass and paperboard plants ended also.

As a result, the socialistic phase of the developmental program terminated with the sale of all five enterprises. The shoe factory was sold to a United States firm in California and the four others were purchased as a package deal by the wealthy Ferré family of Ponce for an attractive $10.5 million. Although Luis Alberto Ferré had opposed the public concept of Operation Bootstrap, he contended later, "I really put the program on its feet."

Thus we find that despite the presence of the supposedly radical team of Tugwell and Muñoz, the Puerto Rican revolution turned out to be ideologically mild. Tugwell had assisted in the agricultural take-over by the government as well as in other areas. Now, Muñoz, despite his early socialistic ideas, was becoming a hardheaded pragmatist willing to take whatever course necessary to bring about greater social justice.

In addition to the liquidation of the publicly owned manufacturing plants, the government now encouraged private business by various incentives, including a law allowing industries certain tax exemptions. After 1947 the attractions offered to manufacturers were specifically these: exemption from income taxes for a specified number of years, a plentiful and cheap labor supply and aid from an organization which had gained worldwide recognition for its capable assistance.

The transitory stage was also characterized by governmental construction of factories and plants for private concerns and especially the signing of a contract for the building and operation of a Conrad Hilton luxury hotel. It was this changed program that acquired the name "Operation Bootstrap." Considered in its utilitarian framework, however, it really began with the governmental program of the Popular Party after 1940, and its concern for the problems of all the people including the forgotten *jíbaro.*

The success of the Conrad Hilton hotel clearly indicates the nature of the program. Until the Caribe Hilton opened for business in 1949, fewer than 60,000 tourists visited Puerto Rico annually. Expenditures by tourists had never exceeded $6.5 million. In ten years the annual tourist inflow increased to 350,000 with an expenditure of $53 million annually. The construction of other hotels was encouraged and soon many bordered San Juan's shoreline as well as other places including Ponce, Mayagüez, and Fajardo.

Caribe Hotel soon reimbursed the government for its investment and also provided the government with a profit running into the millions. A new way of life had arrived on the island and its various ramifications affected the life style of many in a beneficial manner.

Operation Bootstrap has continued to be successful. Industrial development in Puerto Rico has proceeded in four stages: 1) before 1930 manufacturing meant a *central* or a sugar mill, a cigar wrapping factory or children and housewives sewing handkerchiefs and/or gloves in the hills of the interior; 2) beginning in the 1930's and continuing in the 1940's the government endeavored to build and operate its own plants for key products; 3) in the 1950's the government encouraged private business through special construction and tax incentives; 4) since 1960 there has been more emphasis on capital investment in heavy industry, especially petroleum and chemicals. In the late 1960's newspaper headlines played up the possibility of future copper mining in the rugged mountain country of the northwest.

Regardless of the ideology followed, Puerto Rico has made progress. By 1955 income from industry and manufacturing surpassed agriculture. By 1958 some 500 new factories had been added to the economy and over 650 were added a few years later. In 1968 Puerto Rico's Gross National Product was valued at $3.7 billion compared with $755 million in 1950—a growth rate of 9.3 percent per annum. Per capita income rose steadily from $279.00 in 1950 to $1,129.00 in 1968. These gains can be attributed to 1,700 new manufacturing enterprises and approximately 100,000 new jobs.[6]

This progress is matched by similar increases in other areas including world trade, power production, banking activity, and communications and transportation.

On a per capita basis, Puerto Ricans buy more from the United States than citizens of America's biggest customer, Canada, and on an aggregate basis more than some huge countries such as Brazil. The United States in turn is Puerto Rico's best trading partner. The value of Commonwealth shipments to continental United States rose to $302 million in 1953, $452 million in 1958, and to $1,256 million in 1968. This, of course, reflects increased expansion and diversification of the island's production.

The dramatic growth of trade with the United States is equaled by commerce indicating Puerto Rico's increasing global significance. Commonwealth exports to foreign countries increased from $6 million a decade ago to $84 million in 1968; imports, from $23 million to $385 million during the same period.[7]

The agency central to the whole program is the Planning Board created originally in 1942 when Tugwell was governor. Its responsibility is to visualize the total needs. A measure of its service is the increase in electric power provided by the Bootstrap program. From 130 million kilowatt hours in 1940 the amount produced increased to 6,200 million by 1968. This is expected to double in the next decade or so.

In 1942 a Government Development Bank was created to provide medium and long-term loans to promote the economy of Puerto Rico. Up to 1968 the bank had dispersed $167 million for such diverse purposes as construction and expansion of industry, development of tourist facilities as well as money aid for supermarkets, agricultural enterprises, and housing.

All of these developments have served to raise the tempo of general economic activity. In 1959 there were, for example, 64,000 telephones; by June, 1969, that number had increased to 260,000. Overseas telephone service had also increased and has been strained to the limit.

With one automobile for every five persons, Puerto Rico ranks sixth in the world of car ownership. On weekdays San Juan's traffic jams cause some suburbanites to leave home at sunrise to avoid the crunch. If the present growth trend continues, the only solution would be to "add a second floor to the island."

In 1969 Puerto Rico's Gross National Product reached approximately $4 billion, far greater than its Caribbean neighbors: Cuba ($2.5 billion), Dominican Republic ($1.1 billion), and Haiti ($341 million).

The leaders of the Popular Party have been concerned with more than material progress, however. An extremely sensitive measure of the general tone or feeling of a society is the suicide rate. In 1936 it was very high, 30.7 per 100,000, but by 1946 it had dropped to 25.4 and by 1960 it was down to 9.7 per 100,000. Puerto Rico's achievements in the field of education and health have also improved considerably. Illiteracy dropped from 31.5 percent in 1940 to less than 15 percent in 1970, and most illiterates are now in the older generation bracket.

Life expectancy at birth was 46 years in 1940 and today it is over 70 years. This is comparable to the United States standard and much higher than many underdeveloped countries where the range is from 35 to 45 years.

In other words, Puerto Ricans are living longer and eating better, and their homes are better built. But Muñoz has warned his people that "man does not not live by bread alone." Possibly the desire for material gain has placed the dollar sign on a culture once characterized more by love, laughter, music, and poetry. Therefore, Muñoz in his later years has tried to promote the concept of "Operation Serenity" which tends to stress an outlook that would bring the good life, a deep feeling for the essential dignity and worth of each human being regardless of race, color, religion, wealth, or position.

All of the above developments probably explain why Puerto Rico's image has changed considerably since 1930. No longer is the island called Uncle Sam's sweatshop and thought of as a place of no natural resources or advantages. In 1959, for example, it was chosen as the headquarters for the 51st annual meeting of state governors—the first governors' conference held outside the continental United States. In the fall of 1971 the governors met again in San Juan to enjoy *La Isla Verde*.

Will Operation Bootstrap result in some sort of world utopia? No one would question the need, especially if we consider the wants of many of the nations emerging from the abuses of colonialism. Can Puerto Rico serve as a model or an "American showcase" for others to imitate? Before one passes final judgment, it should be pointed out that certain aspects of colonialism remain in the Puerto Rican-Continental United States relationship—advantages and disadvantages. Some 1.5 million Puerto Ricans live in the United States and in some years 50,000 migrate to the mainland. Could the island cope with its population problem if this were not true? In various aids and grants, migrants' remittances, veterans' compensations, social security payments, Puerto Rico acquires from the continental United States what amounts in purchasing power to about 10 percent of the Commonwealth's product.

In working out its future, what form of political status will serve not only the Puerto Ricans, but the people of the entire troubled world as well? Will it be a society which values "a man more for that which he intends to do than that for which he intends to acquire," or will it represent a vulgar, materialistic life style where "the bar has replaced the book as the status symbol"?

Possibly the greatest achievement of the two reformers was the creation of the *Estado Libre Asociado*. Tugwell classified it as remarkable, the greatest tour de force of the Muñoz period. "His Commonwealth had, I really believe, a genuine claim to be rated as a first-rate political device—one to be ranked with our federal Union and with the British Commonwealth."[8]

The description appears apt because it met the demands of the time. As an instrument it brought a greater measure of social justice to all Puerto Ricans and also extended to them a degree of local autonomy. It should also be stressed that this accomplishment was the work of two reformers representing distinct cultures. Tugwell taught the Puerto Ricans efficiency in government, and Muñoz reformed the local political structure in such a manner that a more decent and honest government resulted. Located in the midst of Latin American turbulence, such a creative influence might in truth cause Puerto Rico to become a true "crossroads of the Americas," and as such an inspiration for other troubled regions.

From 1898 on many Puerto Ricans felt they should be treated in accordance with the stipulations of the Northwest Ordinance, as we have already indicated, and that in due time they should be permitted to become a state. The extremists demanded independence. Obviously some alternative must be found. Theodore Roosevelt, Jr., as one of the best-loved of the earlier governors, apparently tried to find a solution to the perplexing choice between independence or statehood. He valued the Puerto Rican cultural background and characteristics and wished to make *La Isla Verde* a connecting link between two cultures as well as a "show window looking south."

Very early Governor Tugwell indicated that political power and effective administration should be lodged in the hands of Puerto Ricans. Financial management or the control of the budget was surely one of the important attributes of power. Previously, governors, in failing to use their veto power properly, had allowed this important function to slip unduly under the influence of the Auditor. Tugwell immediately changed this.

Shortly after taking office he informed the Auditor, Patrick J. Fitzsimmons, that the budget he had prepared for 1942–43 was being discarded and would be revised by the governor himself. Tugwell now turned the problem of finance over to one of the young experts he had brought from the mainland. This young man was Louis Sturche, Jr. Although the budget was revised upward, it was accepted by the 1942 legislature. It was also a financial statement more in line with the real needs of Puerto Rico. Naturally, Fitzsimmons opposed the move and criticized it. Tugwell, however, was backed strongly by Secretary of the Interior Ickes in this move and as a result Fitzsimmons resigned, May 27, 1943. The new Auditor became Rafael de J. Cordera, and the fact that he was Puerto Rican and an independent breathed new life into the office.

Tugwell also realized that such important powers as the appointment of leading officials and control of money should not only be in the hands of the governor, but a governor who truly represented the people. As early as 1942, he informed the President that as a result of various investigations, the Organic Act of Puerto Rico should be amended to convert the governorship into an elective office. Furthermore, he felt that the important executive offices, Auditor, Commissioner of Education, and Attorney General, as well as Supreme Court Justices, should be appointees of the local governor. Democracy could not develop to its full potential in Puerto Rico until legal responsibility and political power were in the same hands. The tragedy of the past decades had been ineffective leadership in times of emergency.

> . . . It is my incidental belief that there will not be one [effective executive] until the [Jones] Act is rewritten to prescribe as one of the Governor's qualifications that he must be a citizen of Puerto Rico as well as of the United States and that he must be elected by the other citizens of the island.[9]

In Tugwell's opinion such a change could bring about an atmosphere that would reduce the evil of too much power politics and thus stop executive strangulation.[10]

In the elections of 1944, as we have noted, Muñoz minimized the issue of political status and strove instead for freedom associated with equality and social justice. According to Tugwell, his "Commonwealth" idea was a neat political trick. Muñoz eventually showed Puerto Ricans how they could have their cake and eat it too. They could rid themselves of "foreigners" and yet get much of the same assistance which went to mainland states. As citizens they received Social Security benefits, as well as federal aid for the building of roads, hospitals, airports, and low-cost housing. Furthermore, they paid no federal income taxes. Having one's cake and eating it too seemed possible with the proper political setup.

This reform, like others, was achieved with the cooperation of both reformers—Tugwell and Muñoz. After the United States mid-term elections of 1946 resulted in a Republican capture of Congress, Tugwell's assets as governor were outweighed by his liabilities. To his credit, he realized this and resigned in 1946.[11] President Truman then appointed the first Puerto Rican as governor, Jesús T. Piñero, a close intimate of Muñoz and an original *Popular*. All this paved the way for the Elective Governor Act of 1947 which amended the Jones Act so that the governor could "be elected by the other citizens of the Island." Some grievances remained, but this seminal change made possible the election of Muñoz Marín in 1948. Moreover, the vote was a landslide for the *Populares* who received 392,356 votes to 89,441 for Republican Statehood group. The Independents came in third with 65,351 votes.

The islanders rejoiced at having Senator Muñoz as their governor; they also appreciated the fact that finally the Popular Party had taken a definite stand on status by espousing *Estado Libre Asociado*, or what amounted to commonwealth status. Some of Muñoz's ex-colleagues viewed this as "traitorous." It was whispered by some, however, that independence was merely in suspense; when Puerto Rico had gotten all possible advantage from commonwealth status, it would demand independence—but with a subsidy; in other words "divorce with alimony."

At any rate, no disaster resulted. Muñoz was elected and reelected until the 1964 election when to the surprise of many he refused to run for the office again. Apparently he did not wish to be considered indispensable.

In March, 1949, the Resident Commissioner to the United States Congress proposed a bill authorizing the people of Puerto Rico "to organize a government pursuant to a constitution of their own adoption," to become effective if approved by the people of Puerto Rico as well as by the Congress.

In a referendum of June, 1951, in which 65 percent of qualified voters participated, the people of Puerto Rico approved Public Law #600 by a margin of 4 to 1. Later in the same year, the people elected 92 delegates to a constitutional convention. After a six-month session a draft was worked out which was also submitted to and approved by popular referendum March 3, 1952. The three main parties participated, but the Independence group chose to withdraw. The vote on July 25, 1952, was 375,000 to 83,000 for the *Estado Libre Asociado*. It was a definite victory for Muñoz and the commonwealth idea; it was also the 54th anniversary of the American take-over.

But there was considerable dissatisfaction. In working out the final document for Congressional approval, the Puerto Ricans tried to reserve the right to "propose and accept modifications" to the constitution. This statement was clear. When, however, Congress changed the bill of rights section to read "aims" of education, fair standards of living, jobs, and other social factors, rather than "rights," a shadow was cast over the whole affair. As a result, friendship between Jaime Benítez, University of Puerto Rico Rector, who had written the bill of rights, and Muñoz cooled somewhat.

In his later years as governor, both in the United States and in Puerto Rico, Muñoz reiterated his belief in the commonwealth idea: "I believe in the Commonwealth.—It provides our people with more political liberty than federated statehood; it ensures far more economic freedom than separate independence; it sets free our cultural personality."[12]

Numerous Puerto Ricans, including both statehooders and *independentistas*, have steadfastly maintained that *La Isla Verde* is still a colony and subject to the unilateral power of Congress. On the contrary, Muñoz has consistently held that the Puerto Rican-United States relationship is a real "compact" which can be changed by mutual agreement only. It all depends, as Humpty Dumpty would put it, on just what the word means.[13] The present arrangement is surely a unique understanding. Undoubtedly Chief Justice Earl Warren had this in mind when he spoke at the inauguration of the Commonwealth Supreme Court building in San Juan, February 4, 1956:

> In the sense that our American system is not static, in the sense that it is not an end but a means to an end—in the sense that it is an organism intended to grow and expand to meet varying conditions and times in a large country—in the sense that every government effort of ours is an experiment—so the new institutions of the Commonwealth of Puerto Rico represent an experiment—the newest experiment and perhaps the most notable of American government experiments in our lifetime.[14]

Such reasoning and the record of Operation Bootstrap as well as of *Estado Libre Asociado* since 1952 seem to justify the optimistic faith of Muñoz that: "Hope is the first ingredient of a peoples' creativeness."

Part III

Puerto Ricans and the Mainland

CHAPTER 8

Migration

CRITICS OF OPERATION BOOTSTRAP CONTEND THAT WHILE PROFITS resulting from tax-free investment of American firms brought some relief to the depressed island people, the increased economic largesse was not equitably distributed, leaving the majority of Puerto Rico's millions in poverty. Instead of fostering healthy economic growth, the United States has been condemned by some for perpetuating economic dependency and thus deepening the cycle of poverty. In substantiating this claim, opponents cite migration figures as proof that the problems of the island were far from solved. A recent article in *Ramparts,* entitled "Puerto Rico: Our Backyard Colony," summarizes this view:

Over one million *boriqueños* have left their native land for the *barrios* of East Harlem and South Bronx. That one-third of a nation would escape into exile to the slums of New York testifies to the living conditions in the Caribbean "paradise."

Four out of every five Puerto Rican families earn less than $3,000.00 per year; one half receive less than $1,000.00 annually. Oscar Lewis puts unemployment at 14 percent; knowledgeable Puerto Ricans insist that a figure as high as 30 percent is more realistic. That is a permanent condition twice as bad as the depths of the Great Depression in this country. Per capita income in Mississippi, our poorest state, was 81 percent higher than in Puerto Rico in 1960. Whereas wages are a fraction of those on the mainland, the cost of living on the island is higher. Most statistics place island costs at 25 percent higher than those in New York, Chicago or Boston.[1]

Although no list of sources is provided and some of the figures are open to question, it would be wise, in view of such assertions, to consider the phenomenon of Puerto Rican migration in greater depth.

There exist three general patterns of movement in connection with Puerto Rico and the United States. Historically, the first movement of people involved migration of United States continentals to Puerto Rico. The second is the movement of Puerto Ricans to the United States beginning shortly after the American occupation but not in significant numbers until the 1940's. Finally, the third general demographic movement involves internal migration within the island—rural to urban as a result of increased industrialization of the island's economy.

The movement of the early continental Americans[2] has been mentioned. After 1898 more appeared and they were not poverty-stricken. On the contrary, the North American who chose to make his home in Puerto Rico usually possessed the technical ability and/or capital to be included in the upper or upper-middle social strata. While tourism is not synonymous with migration, it does represent an influx of aliens into a different environment. As suggested earlier, tourism is characterized by both advantages and disadvantages. All too often, sad to say, comments like the following are true:

> Nor has the more recent upsurge of tourism brought deeper mutual understanding. For the tourist anywhere is rarely interested in enlarging his mental boundaries; he wants to be entertained, not instructed. Also, the American tourist in Puerto Rico comes from a selective social background not representative of the American people . . .[3]

In 1957, for example, 54 percent of the flow into San Juan came from families with rather large incomes. Once this type of tourist reaches the island he has little desire to stray beyond the popular hotels, organized trips, and night clubs. He usually cares little about speaking Spanish. Tourist trade statistics tell us little about the actual conditions in the host country (except that perhaps the scenery is beautiful and that the government is considered "stable") but more about the life style of the tourists themselves.

The influx of Puerto Ricans to the mainland presents an entirely different story and can only be understood in light of its historical setting. This migration is a complex issue as regards its impact on developmental planning because it involves two cultures attempting to come to terms with such complex social phenomena as assimilation, acculturation, saturation, and dispersal, to mention only a few. Puerto Rican migration to the continental United States falls into three main periods: 1) migration prior to the Second World War, 2) the Second World War and immediate postwar period, and 3) a period of gradual stabilization in the 1950's and 1960's, and the increase in "return migration."

The first significant movement out of Puerto Rico occurred during the 1890 s, to Hawaii, as a result of a promotion by the sugar interests of that island. Today, there are approximately 10,000 resident Puerto Ricans in Hawaii. Sidney W. Mintz provides us with an interesting study of the adjustment problems of this group. He concludes that the lack of Puerto Rican advancement from the lower socioeconomic strata is due to competition with more highly organized family groups (for example, the Chinese and Japanese), and perhaps to a gradual hardening of the trend of upward mobility due to discrimination and generally tightening economic conditions.[4] Although sporadic attempts to recruit Puerto Rican labor for agricultural work in the United States during the early decades of the twentieth century met with little response, the 1910 census found Puerto Ricans living in thirty-nine states, and Hawaii. By 1920 only four states had no Puerto Ricans. Subsequent censuses show that after 1920 all states could claim Puerto Rican residents—even sub-arctic Alaska with 562 in 1960.[5]

During the period between the First and Second World Wars, a small number of migrants made their way to the United States, the Virgin Islands, and to various Latin American republics.

NUMBER OF PERSONS BORN IN PUERTO RICO AND LIVING IN THE
CONTINENTAL UNITED STATES AT CENSUS DATES AND IN 1935[6]

Year	Number	Increase
1910	1,513	
1920	11,811	10,298
1930	52,774	40,963
1935	58,200	5,426

One of the major reasons for the reluctance of Puerto Ricans
to migrate to neighboring islands of the West Indies or to other
Latin American nations, with whom they share close cultural
affinity, is the inability to compete with native labor. Wages in
these countries are sometimes lower than those of Puerto Rico
and the standard of living is, in many instances, worse than
in Puerto Rico.

Of the small number of Puerto Ricans living in the United
States prior to the Second World War, the majority were located
in New York. According to the 1930 census, New York had 500
persons of Puerto Rican birth in 1910; 7,000 in 1920; 45,000
in 1930. Although this group included some professional people,
the majority were unskilled workers. The center of settlement was
East Harlem, from 97th Street as far as 125th Street, from Fifth
Avenue to Third Avenue. Three-quarters of the Puerto Ricans
lived in Manhattan where they encountered, to the East, the
old East Harlem Italian community, and the growing community of Negroes to the north and west.[7]

The 1940 New York (Standard Metropolitan Statistical Area)
census recorded 70,000 Puerto Ricans still concentrated predominantly in East Harlem, with a community in Brooklyn
along the waterfront and a small group in the Bronx.[8]

The war period, 1941–1945, interrupted passenger movements.
There was only a small addition to the Puerto Rican population
until 1945. Then the war ended and the results were explosive.
"In 1945, 13,500 entered the city (New York City); in 1946,
almost 40,000.[9] New York suffered the impact of a mass migra-

tion. Gothamites were acutely aware of this most recent barrage of strangers. The sensationalist and xenophobic reactions of the press, as well as what the social scientists call the "factor of higher visibility," are well illustrated by many newspaper articles.[10]

One daily headline in 1946, for example, read "Tidal Wave of Puerto Ricans Swamping City." It was pointed out that the net migration in 1945 was 13,573 but had reached 39,911 in 1946. Another example would be the claimed total for New York City which was put at 710,000 in 1948, when it was actually about 180,000. A few years later another paper reported "there are an esimated 2,000,000 Puerto Ricans living in the nation's largest city." That year, 1953, the true count approximated 450,000 if 100,000 born of Puerto Ricans were counted. Such inaccuracies are understood and termed "perceptual accentuation" by the social scientist. But even the "professionals" were apparently guilty of gross distortion.

Workers in one agency estimated their Puerto Rican case load at 75 percent of all clients. They were greatly surprised when they were told the correct proportion was 30 percent. Frequently, estimates even by professionally trained personnel ran two to three times the real figure.[11]

From 1940 to 1960 an estimated total of 600,000 native-born Puerto Ricans migrated to the United States. The two most frequently quoted sources are the United States Bureau of the Census, the census for 1960, and the Commonwealth of Puerto Rico, Department of Labor, Migration Division.[12] The number of persons of Puerto Rican birth residing in the United States at the time of the 1960 census was computed to be 617,056. In 1940, the Census had recorded 69,967. These figures indicate an increase of 547,089 migrants. According to the Commonwealth's Department of Labor, Migration Division, the net migration between 1946 and 1956 was 458,074. Adding to this figure the airport survey of the Commonwealth's Department of Labor,

Bureau of Labor Statistics, for the years 1957, 1958, and 1959, a total of 631,474 is obtained. These figures do not take into account the "floating population" which would probably place the number somewhere between 600,000 and 700,000.[13]

The next questions which arise are: What caused such a people to move? What factors influenced the migrant to leave his homeland and attempt to make a place for himself in unfamiliar and often hostile areas? In essence what are the "push" and "pull" factors?

As mentioned earlier, one of the most outstanding characteristics of the Puerto Rican populace is their exploding birth rate. Improvement in the hospital facilities and other means of public health since the beginning of the twentieth century and the added impetus given such projects under Operation Bootstrap have not contributed markedly to a decline in the birth rate. This density of population poses severe socioeconomic pressure on the island's resources.

For example, Hormigueros, a small town in southeast Puerto Rico, now has no space to bury its dead. A few empty graves are reserved but urban sprawl prevents an expanding cemetery; consequently the dead of that small village are taken elsewhere. This place might be termed a microcosm of the island's spiraling population problem. It took some 400 years after Columbus discovered the island for the population to reach one million. In 1971 the total approached three million and many Puerto Ricans are in the United States. The population will probably double witthin the next 35 years. This is largely due to better health measures which have cut infant mortality and increased life expectancy greatly. Now, there is an approximate natural increase of 50,000 persons per year.[14]

Thus, overcrowding on the island appears to be one of the main "push" factors in motivating the prospective migrant. However, expanding population is not the only reason for migration. Closely related are the considerations of economic opportunity and social mobility. Puerto Rico's upper classes are called *blanquitos* ("little whites") by the poor. Although this term denotes more of a cultural distinction than a racial one (for instance, the poor whites use this term), it cannot be denied that Anglo-Saxon cultural standards have enhanced the racial distinctions among Puerto Ricans.

Most American continentals are white and wealthier than the average Puerto Rican; consequently, success is expected with whiteness. The Spaniards, too, were white and usually more affluent, but they tolerated and often entered into interracial marriage. However, most Americans have tried to continue their continental life style.

A United States Civil Liberties Commission reported in 1958 that racial tension in Puerto Rico was not "critical" but that an intolerant attitude brought from the United States had undoubtedly influenced the island negatively. Many blacks were quoted as saying they were "uncomfortable" in social gatherings full of white people. When white families were asked whether they would object to a daughter marrying a Puerto Rican, about half said yes, but only a few stated they would forcibly prohibit such a union.[15]

One must, however, use caution in citing racial criteria as factors in social mobility on the island. The situation is not the same as found on the American continent, as witnessed by the numerous cases of men of color who have achieved success, such as Luis Negrón López, an "Indian-ish *trigueño*" (brown), who was for many years the Puerto Rican Senate Majority Leader (and ran for the governorship in 1968); Ernest Ramos Antonini, the late Speaker of the Puerto Rican House of Representatives; and José Celso Barbosa (1857–1921), a black M.D. who served in the cabinet of the autonomous government in 1897, as Undersecretary of Education, and later became the founder of the Statehood Republican Party.

Perhaps it would be more accurate to consider Puerto Rican insular mobility in terms of socioeconomic potential rather than racial patterns. This is what the "Black Power" advocate, Stokely Carmichael, attempted when, during his visit in 1967, he minimized the racial issue and attacked United States colonialism. Even though many of the factors which contribute to racial tension on the continent are absent, and it appears that the rigid class structure of the countryside has been broken, a member of the lowest class—the *jíbaro*—rarely follows in the steps of Horatio Alger. While some mobility of the lower classes is evident, the slow rate of upward movement combined with the burgeoning population presents a critical situation. In response to this dilemma, out-migration acts as a safety valve in social mobility as its siphons off the excessive labor supply. An ever-increasing number of families face housing shortages and slum conditions in Puerto Rico. Building costs have skyrocketed despite government efforts to accelerate and subsidize low-cost housing projects. Families with moderate incomes must increasingly locate at the fringe of the suburbs. The financing now represents 34 percent of a new home's cost (double the United States average), and in 1972 the cheapest private homes cost about $16,300.00. Today only one family in five has an annual income to qualify for a mortgage under these prices.

Puerto Rican slum conditions are actually no worse than those of other Latin American countries; but because of Puerto Rico's unique relationship with the United States—the epitome of opulence and prosperity—poverty becomes more difficult to bear. In Puerto Rico a slum is called an *arrabal*. These are clustered in a helter-skelter fashion around the greater metropolitan areas, thus emphasizing contrasts between the city which is to the poor a symbol of opportunity, progress, and the hope of advancement, and the conditions existing in the disadvantaged areas. Puerto Rico's worst slum borders the Martín Peña Channel of San Juan Bay. In this backwater live 71,000 people. The Martín Peña slum claims the highest rates of infant mortality, welfare cases, tuberculosis, pneumonia, delinquency, and violence in the San Juan area. A second and perhaps more famous slum—*La Perla* ("The Pearl")—is vividly described as a slum bordering Old San Juan and as being elegant in comparison with Martín Peña.

La Perla, separated from the main city by colonial fortifications, has been termed a labyrinthine Caribbean Casbah of 900 houses with a population of roughly 3,500. The beach is strewn with filth and garbage which serves ideally for the pigs which the poor raise to supplement their diet. The constant trade-wind breeze helps eliminate a stench which otherwise would be overwhelming.

El Fanguito, another San Juan slum district, has been mentioned previously.

The final element which will be considered under the category of "push" factors is the Puerto Rican government's publicizing of opportunities for would-be migrants to the continental United States.

Denials to the contrary, the Puerto Rican government has been a promoter of migration to the United States as one alternative to the problem of over-population, especially of those who might be classified as "part of the labor market." The Migration Division of the Commonwealth Labor Department has offices in nine eastern and midwestern American cities. These serve as the middlemen between prospective employers and workers. They negotiate contracts which guarantee a fixed minimum wage, decent working conditions, and round-trip air fare. Seasonal farm labor on United States fruit, vegetable, and tobacco farms generally earns from $1.50 to $1.75 per hour. Approximately 40,000 migrant workers per year, however, are clandestinely working without a legal contract.[16]

Nine Puerto Rican employment offices assist in recruiting and preparing laborers for work in the United States. Using labor market information gathered from United States employment services in the United States, agencies aid in placement and in the supervision of local employment-orientation committees located in all sizeable Puerto Rican towns. The media—television, radio, and brochures—spread the message of economic opportunity on the mainland. The government sponsors the printing and distribution of millions of leaflets which are simply written, attractively illustrated and deal with such subjects as the urgency of knowing English, climate and clothing in the States, the documents which are needed for schools and other institutions, the need for a driver's license . . . warnings . . . and a wide variety of other topics.[17]

In fact, the Puerto Rican government's promotion of migration as a panacea for the population crisis has been criticized as a stop-gap measure—not only tying the Puerto Rican economy to the fluctuations of the United States labor market, but also contributing to many of the adjustment problems of the incompletely acculturated Puerto Rican immigrant.

So vital is the flow of migrants to the continent for the low-standard island economy that it apparently acts as a safety valve. Moreover, it is not difficult to believe the charges made by critics such as Adam Clayton Powell in 1959 that the commonwealth government was not too assiduous in advising its citizens of the hardship conditions awaiting them on the streets of New York or in the harvest fields of New Jersey, Indiana, or Connecticut. Efforts by Washington to curb the flow by putting Puerto Ricans on a quota system could have only disastrous consequences. Regardless of the blame, it is undoubtedly true that several hundred thousand Puerto Ricans reside in New York who cannot speak English and this casts doubt upon the efficacy of commonwealth government's program relative to migrants. "The island worker truly benefits from his freedom of movement within the American economy, but he remains its hewer of wood and drawer of water. He may not hate America as a result, yet he has little reason to love it."[18]

Obviously, the "pull" factor of major importance is that of economic gain. One of the best indicators of the pull effect of the United States economy on Puerto Rican labor migration is the study by Clarence Senior which graphically correlates the volume of Puerto Rican migration with the expansion and contraction of the national economy. For example, there was a net reverse flow of Puerto Rican migration during the depressions of 1907–1909, 1920–1921, and in the 1930's, and a decreased percentage of migration during the slumps of 1948–1949, 1953–1954, 1957–1958, and 1963; while increased demand for labor gave rise to a new migration increase in 1955–1956, 1959, 1962–1963, reaching its peak during the early 1950's. Thus the Puerto Rican, like many immigrants before him, came with the hope of economic improvement and with dreams of a better life. Migration, in general, rose in response to labor shortages on the continent and improved transportation, connecting supply with demand.

The element of cheap transportation is of crucial importance, since a round-trip ticket can be purchased for about $90. Home is merely a few hours' flight time away. Bargain transportation has enabled United States labor contractors to rely on an adequate and dependable supply of cheap labor. Moreover, such a labor supply is apparently vital to the economic development of many areas in the United States, especially some eastern states. For example, the Harvard New York Metropolitan Region Study announced that: "The rate of Puerto Rican migration to New York is one of the factors that determine how long and how successfully the New York metropolitan region will retain industries which are under competitive pressure from other areas."[19]

Closely associated with cheap transportation is the element of relative freedom of movement enjoyed by the *Puertoriqueños*. The absence of legal restrictions because of American citizenship is in contrast to the more stringent immigration quotas and qualifications of other neighboring countries. (Some Latin American countries have strict and almost prohibitive immigration policies). Puerto Rican migration to the United States is technically one of "internal" migration. Because of its character, the migrant is subject to very little inspection or regulation and may travel as freely as a citizen of any state of the Union.

Another and very strong "pull" factor is the familial tie. The institution of the extended family plays an important role in promoting increased migration. Often the family in Puerto Rico was broken by the desire of the first members to explore the opportunities offered by the Statue of Liberty image. This usually meant hardship—the selling of household goods and belongings—to meet the cost of transportation. In prosperous years it was usually easier for the woman to secure work. She could live with friends, learn the conditions of the country, and save some money. Arrangements could then be made for other members of the family to follow: "Finally, the father, or husband might come. . . . Since according to all of the social workers and others who are in close contact with the group in New York, it is customary for Puerto Ricans to share whatever they have with relatives to migrate. . . ."[20] Thus, most often, the migrant comes to the United States in response to an opportunity secured for him by relatives already established within the country. This factor helps explain the high proportion of Puerto Rican settlements in the New York area, where the majority of the Puerto Rican population is located (970,000 in 1970 according to the statistics of the Office of the Commonwealth).[21]

Finally, the labor recruitment activities of continental business concerns cannot be overlooked. In cooperation with the Puerto Rican Department of Labor, the United States Department of Labor provides employment referral services, information about local laws and customs, and works closely with such public and private institutions as schools, settlement houses, churches, labor unions, and other governmental agencies. Private interests engage in extensive labor promotion activities, but they must conform to the standards of fair employment set by the Federal Government. However, each year numerous cases of fraud and illegal hiring are exposed. In conjunction with the Puerto Rican Department of Labor, Migration Division, the United States Labor Department encourages and finances special orientation programs which will be discussed later.

Any treatment of Puerto Rican migration to the continental United States is not complete without some mention of the reverse phenomenon—"return migration." Most indices show that return migration takes place during periods of labor saturation and general economic contraction. The recent trend has been one of increased return migration, beginning in earnest during the mid-1960's and continuing until the present. It has already been mentioned that between the years 1955 and 1963 an estimated 83,000 Puerto Ricans returned to *La Isla Verde*. This is a complex phenomenon which not only involves economic but also sociocultural questions. Most social scientists feel that this return migration is partially due to a failure of a portion of the Puerto Rican population to adjust successfully to American life. (The problems involved in acculturation and adaptation will be discussed in the following chapters). Improved conditions on the island, the Puerto Rican government's recently increased efforts to attract skilled labor, and the Puerto Ricans' love for their homeland are other factors which must be taken into account.

The third and final category of Puerto Rican migration is the intra-island movement. Most generally this entails migration from a rural to an urban setting. Internal migration differs in scope from emigration, yet the patterns are similar. With the application of technology to agriculture, the average annual rural employment was 90,000 in 1964, considerably less than in 1940. This is substantiated by the fact that the rural population shows heaviest losses in the coffee regions and the eastern offshore islands. Since most of the industrial development takes place in urban areas, the natural tendency has been a general movement from the country to the city.

The decade 1930–1940 saw 54 of 77 *municipios* losing some population. Thirty-three lost about 10 percent of their 1930 figure and six lost 20 percent or more. Data does not seem to be available for the next period, but the 1950–1960 decade showed a loss of 10 percent of the 1950 population for 39 *municipios*. Several areas, such as Bayamon, Carolina, Catano, Trujillo Alto, gained, but these were all part of the larger metropolitan region.

There are now 55 cities in Puerto Rico, compared with 17 in 1899. The urban proportion of the population has risen as follows:[22]

	Percent
1899	14.6
1910	20.1
1920	21.8
1930	27.7
1940	30.3
1950	40.5
1960	44.2

The Puerto Rican migration was unlike the movement of Europeans to the western hemisphere who were spurred by the same but other factors as well. The *jíbaro* was not running away from religious persecution, forced military service, or even political discrimination after 1940. Herman Badillo, first continental Puerto Rican to be elected to the United States House of Representatives, concludes, "The migration of Puerto Ricans to the mainland is not for political or religious reasons, but purely economic . . ."[23] In a real sense the Puerto Ricans came for much the same reasons as the Mexican *bracero* (worker) or the *mojado* (wetback) who crossed the Rio Grande. Besides the economic factor, undoubtedly the Statue of Liberty image held out promises of greater opportunity for all—educational and democratic. Were these expectations to be fulfilled?

CHAPTER 9

Mainland Puerto Ricans and the Diaspora

HISTORICALLY, NEW YORK CITY HAS BEEN HOME TO MOST NEWLY arrived twentieth-century migrants. The Puerto Ricans are no exception to the rule.

Per Cent of Migrants living in New York City[1]

	Number	Percent
1910	554	37
1920	7,364	62
1930	44,908	81
1940	61,463	88
1950	187,420	83
1960	429,710	70

In 1970, 969,700 were reported living in New York (Standard Metropolitan Statistical Area).[2] The choice of New York is a simple one for the Puerto Ricans. Most have relatives who already reside in New York and are willing to provide a place to stay and assist in the search for work. Although this tendency has, to a certain degree, been breaking down, generally a relative or *compadre* is obligated initially to aid the newcomer.

On many occasions the Migration Division of the Department of Labor of Puerto Rico has located jobs for workers—originally in groups of 30 or 40. Soon such small nuclei would grow to a Puerto Rican community of 2,000 to 3,000. Usually the same motives and mechanisms would be found at work. The foreman of a plant, impressed by the productivity of the first workers, might inquire, "Are there more at home like you?"

Shortly a brother, *compadre,* or uncle might appear to fill a vacancy on the line: "The most dramatic illustration known to the authors of the power of this system involves a young mechanic from Lares who went to work in a garage in a small New York town. Within two years, there were about 900 Lareños in that and nearby towns—and they all came from the same barrio!"[3] The fact that the most important trade routes were between New York and San Juan, and improved transportation to New York City, made it more accessible than any other mainland city, are undoubtedly deciding factors in the pattern of settlement. Furthermore, New York City's cosmopolitan outlook modified the extent of racial discrimination anticipated by the newcomers. Finally, the need for unskilled or semiskilled labor drew these expectant people to the numerous jobs which a city of the magnitude of New York can provide.[4]

But not all Puerto Ricans settled in New York City. In fact, it would seem for them to be more logical to locate somewhere in the southern United States where the climate, vegetation, and, to a certain extent, the culture is more similar to that of Puerto Rico. New Mexico, California, Texas, and Florida were subject to Spanish control long before the English gained hegemony.

However, if this proposition is examined more closely, the advantages of locating in the South or Southwest become less obvious. In the first place, the Puerto Rican would have to compete with a large Negro labor force already living at the subsistence level. Secondly, if the Puerto Rican went to the Southwest, he would be invading the job market traditionally filled by Mexican *bracero* labor. Finally, Puerto Ricans feared the more militant racial discrimination characteristic of these areas. In addition to these considerations it must be remembered that during the period of increasing migration, 1922–1930, it was the Eastern and Midwestern urban centers, and not the rural areas of the South or West, that were prospering. The attraction of high money came from the cities, not from farming areas.

week, June 1970, emphasizes the phenomenal growth and spread of Puerto Rican communities:

... the Puerto Rican influence was clearly discernible ... and daily growing more so in scores of cities, towns and villages from Chicago to upstate New York and New England. Today, the Puerto Rican population of Chicago stands at upwards of 100,000. Boston has seen its Puerto Rican population soar from 800 to 25,000 in less than a decade. There are 45,000 in Newark, and in towns like Bridgeport, Connecticut, Rochester, New York, and Dayton, Ohio, such Puerto Rican staples as *plátanos* and *yautías* are commonplace items in super-markets and small grocery stores alike.[7]

Although the early 1960's demonstrate a decline in the net migra-tion, the 1970 census figures support claims of expanding Puerto Rican numbers and influence in the United States.

Puerto Rico: New migration, to and from the coterminous United States, 1944–1965

1944	11,000	1955	45,464
1945	13,000	1956	52,315
1946	39,911	1957	37,704
1947	24,551	1958	27,690
1948	32,775	1959	29,989
1949	25,698	1960	16,298
1950	34,703	1961	−1,754
1951	52,899	1962	11,664
1952	59,103	1963	−5,479
1953	69,124	1964	1,370
1954	21,531	1965	16,678

The minus figures represent a net outflow from the United States to Puerto Rico.[8]

At present several general characteristics of Puerto Rican settlement and geographic mobility can be identified. Firstly, migration from Puerto Rico and interstate migration have tended to shift away from New York City. Writing in the late 1940's,

C. Wright Mills said that New York City seems to have had an image monopoly as to the proper place to go and the island was permeated with influences and lures of that city. Moreover, most of the people who considered leaving the island thought specifically of coming to New York and never considered any other place.[9] Until a few years ago *Nueva York* and the United States were almost synonymous to most Puerto Rican migrants. "Today, four out of ten migrants settle elsewhere on the mainland. Migrants have long been attracted to Bridgeport, Connecticut, mainly due to the region's tobacco crop. The Puerto Rican population there has quadrupled in the past decade and now numbers 150,000.[10] From a study of the 1960 census, José Hernandez-Alvarez in "The Movement and Settlement of Puerto Rican Migrants within the United States, 1950–1960," observed that a shift away from New York City occurred in terms of migration from the island and internal movement between the states. This resulted in the development of major Puerto Rican communities in eight other metropolitan areas of the United States.[11]

Second, the Puerto Rican population has become somewhat mobile within the United States, especially from neighborhood to neighborhood within the same city—usually in the direction of areas marked by out-migration of non-Puerto Ricans.

MOVERS AND MIGRANTS 1948–49 TO 1964–65[12]
(IN THOUSANDS)

| Year | Total | Persons moving their homes | | |
		Within same county	From one county to another in same state	From one state to another
1948–49	27,127	18,792	3,992	4,344
1949–50	27,526	19,276	4,360	3,889
1950–51	31,158	20,694	5,276	5,188
1951–52	29,840	19,874	4,854	5,112
1952–53	30,786	20,638	4,626	5,522

1953–54	29,027	19,046	4,947	5,034
1954–55	31,492	21,086	5,511	4,895
1955–56	33,098	22,186	5,859	5,053
1956–57	31,834	21,566	5,192	5,076
1957–58	33,263	22,023	5,656	5,584
1958–59	32,804	22,315	5,419	5,070
1959–60	33,811	22,564	5,724	5.523
1960–61	35,535	24,289	5,493	5,753
1961–62	34,364	23,341	5,461	5,562
1962–63	35,411	23,059	5,712	6,640
1963–64	36,327	24,089	6,191	6,047
1964–65	37,866	25,122	6,597	6,147

From 1955 to 1960 the percentage of Puerto Ricans in the entire United States engaged in interstate migration was rather low: "Clearly weighed down by the practical absence of interstate mobility toward New York State. When compared with the notably higher rates of interstate mobility outside New York. this finding tends to confirm the pattern of dispersal spoken of above."[13] However, if one compares interstate mobility with migration from Puerto Rico for the first generation, it would appear that direct migration from Puerto Rico has a greater dispersal effect than interstate dispersion once the migrants have reached the mainland. This is not as true for the second generation—those born of Puerto Rican parents—who experience greater interstate mobility.

Third, the trend is increasingly toward the decline of the *colonia* settlement, characterized by high density per tract—the situation in New York City[14]—and the evolution of the *diaspora*. This observation is congruent with the observation of increasing settlement of second-generation Puerto Ricans in areas other than New York City.

A small but widely scattered portion of the Puerto Rican population of the United States (possibly 10 to 15 percent, in 1960) does not live in the residential pattern called *colonia*. This segment could be called the *diaspora* and includes individuals living in about 38 states and 168 metropolitan areas where the total Puerto Rican population may not reach the number found in daytime on a central street corner in New York City or in a neighborhood block at night or at the international airport on a Sunday afternoon.[15]

Since 1940, Puerto Ricans living in the United States have concentrated in the Northeast. Although this region has witnessed a decline in the number of Puerto Rican residents, the Northeast still contains approximately eighty-four percent of those of Puerto Rican origin. The North Central region and the South saw small increases in their percentages of Puerto Rican-born while the West experienced relatively no change.

PERSONS OF PUERTO RICAN BIRTH IN THE UNITED STATES BY REGION:[16]

Region	1940 No.	Pct.	1950 No.	Pct.	1960 No.	Pct.
Total	69,967	100.0	226,110	100.0	615,384	100.0
Northeast	65,059	93.0	200,630	88.7	518,403	84.2
North Central	925	1.3	8,595	3.8	46,611	7.6
South	1,789	2.6	9,720	4.3	31,904	5.2
West	2,194	3.1	7,165	3.2	18,466	3.0

If we examine the Puerto Rican migrant population according to distribution by state, the most obvious fact is the uneven distribution with New York State claiming seventy percent (according to the 1960 census) of all Puerto Rican-born in the United States. New Jersey is next with six percent.[17]

PERSONS OF PUERTO RICAN ORIGIN ON THE UNITED STATES MAINLAND RANKED WITHIN REGIONS BY STATES: 1960[18]

Region & State of Residence	Total Puerto Rican Origin No.	%	Born in Puerto Rico No.	%	Puerto Rican Parentage No.	%
Total U. S.	892,513	100.0	617,056	100.0[a]	275,457	100.0
Northeast	740,813	83.0[b]	518,403	84.0	222,402	80.7
New York	642,622	72.0	448,585	72.7	194,037	70.4

New Jersey	55,351	6.2	39,779	6.4	15,572	5.7
Pennsylvania	21,206	2.4	14,659	2.4	6,547	2.4
Connecticut	15,247	1.7	11,172	1.8	4,075	1.5
Massachusetts	5,217	.6	3,454	.6	1,763	.6
North Central	67,833	7.6	46,611	7.6	21,222	7.7
Illinois	36,081	4.0	25,843	4.2	10,238	3.7
Ohio	13,940	1.6	9,227	1.5	4,713	1.7
Indiana	7,218	.8	4,781	.8	2,437	.9
South	45,,876	5.1	31,904	5.2	13,972	5.1
Florida	19,535	2.2	14,245	2.3	5,290	1.9
Texas	6,050	.7	3,869	.6	2,181	.8
West	38,030	4.3	20,138	3.3	17,892	6.5
California	28,108	3.1	15,479	2.5	12,692	4.6
Hawaii	4,289	.5	1,197	.2	3,092	1.1

a. In many of the tables presented, the percentages do not add up to 100.0 percent. Frequently the sum will be 99.9 or 100.1 percent due to rounding errors involved in carrying percentages to only one decimal place. In such cases, the entry opposite the total is written as 100.0 percent because of the implied generalizing function of percentages. The component percentages have not been changed.

b. States having less than .5 percent of the total Puerto Rican origin population are not presented in this table.

The Puerto Rican population is, for the most part, located in urban areas; ninety-six percent of the Puerto Rican population was classified as urban in the 1960 census.

Regardless of his reasons for coming, regardless of previous orientation experiences, and regardless of his ultimate destination, the Puerto Rican is hit squarely and often harshly with the realization that the continental United States just is not the same as Puerto Rico. In other words—culture shock!

While conditions were bad at home, the migrant's initial experiences in the United States shatter any illusions about America being the land of milk and honey—a land where easy money is made. Granted, the pay is better than on the island, yet, like previous generations of immigrants before him, he is able to afford only the cheapest dwellings in the most rundown neighborhoods.[19] In describing the housing situation and sanitary and health facilities in the areas of major Puerto Rican concentration, John R. Howard in his book *Awakening Minorities* writes:

> About half of all private dwellings in East Harlem are dilapidated. Almost one in three is overcrowded. Tuberculosis rates and venereal disease rates are high. One pregnant woman in three gets no prenatal care and the infant mortality rate is 37 per 1,000 live births as compared to a city average of 26 per 1,000 live births. While 38 percent of blacks and 64 percent of the whites in East Harlem owned their own homes in 1960, few Puerto Ricans did. One in three of East Harlem's Puerto Ricans lives in a "project." Projects are high-rise public housing developments. There are nine in East Harlem.[20]

Glazer and Moynihan concur in their denunciation of the atrocious living conditions in the slums of New York City. However, they find the Puerto Rican settlement pattern unlike that of any previous group.

By 1960 *El Barrio* in East Harlem was only one of the important areas for Puerto Ricans in New York City. An increase in the Puerto Rican population was made impossible in that area by a slum clearance program for public housing. This caused the Puerto Ricans to seek habitations elsewhere and in the late 1940's and 1950's they spread rapidly to the West Side, Washington Heights, Chelsea, the Lower East Side, downtown Brooklyn, Bronx, Melrose, Morrisania, sections of Queens and other districts—even areas in New Jersey: "There was scarcely an area in the older boroughs in which Puerto Ricans were not to be found. Thus because of the housing shortage and slum clearance they rubbed shoulders with everybody in the city."[21] Clarence Senior also notes that the Puerto Rican settlement pattern in New York City has been distinguished by the fact that unlike previous migrants, the Puerto Ricans' geographic mobility has been influenced by American color attitudes. Skin color seems to affect the grouping of Puerto Ricans. A university study conducted in 1948 found much difference between East Harlem,

57 percent white, and the Morrisania area with 77 percent white. If the study had included the regions where the more economically successful Puerto Ricans lived—Washington Heights, Inwood, Queens, Yonkers, and the Long Island suburbs—the differences would undoubtedly have been even greater: "What this proves, of course, is that dark-complexioned people of any origin have difficulties when they try to move out of distinctive 'colored' neighborhoods."[22]

In addition to the housing problem, the newly arrived Puerto Rican immigrant is at a disadvantage because of his lack of skills, particularly his inability to comprehend English. Unlike the early Puerto Rican immigrants who were generally better educated, urbanized, and members of the middle or upper classes, the later, post-World War II migrants, on the whole, were less prepared to cope with the complexities presented by migrating. Possessing fewer resources and skills, the increasing number of lower-class, rural *jíbaros* who migrated filled the lowest-paid positions often considered menial by former Puerto Rican immigrants.

The small number of Puerto Ricans resident in New York prior to the late mass migration did not feel themselves to be a victim of racial prejudice. After immigration became an obvious reality, conditions changed—very markedly. An old resident of Puerto Rico might have said with pride: "I am a Spaniard or Puerto Rican!" All that time migrants from *La Isla Verde* were something strange and exotic: "There weren't enough of them to be a threat to anybody, not enough of them to be identified as a group. The word 'spic' came later (most common theory; from the phrase 'No spik Inglis'). It came with the wave after the war. It came with the airplane."[23] Often only temporary or seasonal work is available to the newcomer who is usually the first to get laid off and the last to be rehired. This is one of the reasons behind the swelling figures of Puerto Rican unemployed and the disproportionate share of Puerto Ricans on relief.

Puerto Ricans are at the bottom of the economic ladder among New York City's ethnic groups. As late as the 1960's white families averaged $8,000.00 per year, non-white (principally black) $5,000.00, while Puerto Ricans were as low as $4,000.00.

In other respects also, Puerto Ricans suffered by comparison with blacks. One director of the Bureau of Labor Statistics indicated that approximately 37 percent of Puerto Rican workers were unemployed. The rate for blacks was lower. In a Brooklyn section the rates ran 29.7 percent for Puerto Ricans and 27.6 percent for blacks. In Harlem it was respectively 12 percent for Puerto Ricans and only 8 percent for blacks.[24] In addition, the Puerto Rican finds himself confronted with the problem of a language barrier which tends to aggravate an often already uncomfortable existence.

How is the Puerto Rican migrant to cope with the problems of unemployment and language? Naturally, he places his hopes in education—if not for himself at least for his children. But in this, too, he encounters frustrations. As a result of unequal educational opportunities and the de facto segregation, coupled with the accompanying slum-enhanced social problems (i.e, dope, delinquency, mental and physical illness, etc.), the Puerto Rican receives an inadequate and often negative education at best. Patricia Sexton after investigating social classes and education in 1965 found that 57 percent of East Harlem's school teachers had permanent licenses, 25 percent were substitutes, 18 percent were probationary. The junior high school was somewhat lower with 44 percent permanent licenses and 43 percent were substitutes. "... In the third grade, students in one district scored 2.8 on a reading test compared with the city average of 3.5. By the eighth grade, the East Harlem students were two full years below grade level.... By the eighth grade their IQ score was 83.2, compared with 103.4 for the city."[25] Only 1.2 percent of graduating Puerto Rican high school seniors receives an "academic diploma" enabling him to enter college. This accounts for the fact that while Puerto Ricans comprise twenty-five percent of the New York public-school population, they constitute barely four percent of the City University's enrollment. Of the remainder who graduate from high school eight percent obtain a vocational degree and the rest a general diploma. Moreover, eight out of ten Puerto Rican children never even complete high school. The situation is universally condemned. Herman Badillo, former Bronx Borough President and now a Congressman from the reshuffled Twenty-first District, declared: "We've already doomed one generation because of the failure of the New York school system."[26] Eften Ramírez, narcotics coordinator in Lindsay's first administration, blamed part of the educational failure on "lack of rôle models . . . for a Puerto Rican kid doesn't see many of his people making it; and until he feels there is a place for him in American society, he's not going to have much interest or faith in school."[27] It should be noted that of New York City's 60,000 school teachers only 400 are of Puerto Rican origin.

Subtle cultural differences such as the change in the roles of the family, while not serious, merely aggravate an often strained situation. Once in New York, the typical migrant might change jobs and homes often. This coupled with layoffs and high-priced housing engenders bitterness. However, most plug on patiently, for conditions were not so rosy in Puerto Rico either. Some get their "second wind" and become established. But for many families problems are numerous and complicated. Children, for example, are hard to discipline and roam the streets and ". . . the wife, now working, may grow too heady for her new-found freedom. In Puerto Rico's countryside, no one is too alarmed if an angry man beats his wife or children. In New York, it is a crime to whip a dog, let alone a human being."[28]

To the previously mentioned conditions which confront the Puerto Rican migrant, a final and most crucial problem must be examined. The problem is racial discrimination. Piri Thomas, Puerto Rican novelist and poet who was himself raised in Spanish Harlem during the 1940's, succinctly sums up the popular belief of those who have suffered from American racism when he writes: "Over here, if you're white you're right, if you're brown, you're wrong, if you're black . . . get back!"[29]

The extent to which the races have mingled in Puerto Rican

history have been noted earlier.[30] What has resulted has been the evolution of a racial attitude quite different from that encountered on the continent. While color discrimination exists on the island, it most often reflects socioeconomic distinction rather than one of race.[31] Both upper and middle classes are considered predominantly white—of Spanish descent—while the lower classes are considered colored. The distinctions are ascriptive—cultural instead of inherited—racial. As the rural laborer or *jíbaro* moves to the city and adjusts to urban life and assumes a more sophisticated life style, he is no longer thought of as primarily black. The difference in color consciousness between Puerto Rico and the mainland may be inferred from the Puerto Ricans' detailed vocabulary used in describing color variations.

Puerto Rican attitudes towards color have been more complicated and less vicious than those of Anglos and this has made their adaptation more difficult. From the Puerto Rican perspective, mainland attitudes on race are simple-minded and malevolent. The Puerto Rican lexicon on color is much richer than that found on the mainland. An individual regarded as a "Negro" by an Anglo might be termed triguero (*sic*), indio, grifo, Hispano, or Negro by a Puerto Rican . . . Their terminology reflects very fine discriminations in terms of skin, color, physiognomy, and hair texture.[32]

Americans, on the other hand, tend to view the world in terms of either black or white. The criterion of colored status is racial and not cultural.

What happens to the migrant in New York where only four percent of the Puerto Ricans are clearly colored? How does the person of "intermediate color" adjust to a society which categorizes him as a black and thus a member of what he considers a lower socioeconomic group? C. Wright Mills in *The Puerto Rican Journey* contends that those falling within this category are the least assimilated.[33] This group passionately identifies with all things Puerto Rican, emphasizing their culture and language in an effort to be distinguished from the American black.

It is this Puerto Rican segment which is most bitter and

blames the simplistic social attitudes for the dilemmas which are encountered. This ambivalent status is a constant source of emotional and psychological frustration which in some instances threatens family unity itself, as the lighter-skinned members are more or less accepted into white society while the darker skinned are rejected. The more militant Puerto Ricans are convinced that white society consciously maneuvers to force Puerto Ricans to remain second-class citizens who are fit only to live in ghettos and work menial jobs and live on a margin of mere subsistence. Voicing such sentiments is Harlem-born filmmaker José García who created an award-winning television documentary on the basis of Piri Thomas's autobiography, *Down These Mean Streets*.[34] García charges that white society's only method of maintaining control is "to divide and conquer the minorities by forcing us to fight each other for the few crumbs it tosses our way."[35]

Relations between Puerto Ricans and American Negro minorities are not exactly cordial. Job competition coupled with Puerto Rican disdain at being considered black—particularly among newly arrived groups of intermediate color—and the tensions, anxieties, and frustration associated with ghetto life combine to form an explosive situation.

Thus the Puerto Rican immigrant faces an increasingly complex American society which often presents problems with which he cannot successfully cope.

. . . The guest is made to understand that he is now in the land of *Tío Samuel* where time is money and labor is not merely an economic means, but also a spiritual necessity. The newcomer must find a job. Since he has no profession or vocational training and has not mastered the language of the country, possibilities of a good job are limited. Again he experiences unemployment, only this time he has other handicaps against him; language and color. He ends up washing dishes, doing janitorial work and, if perchance he should know enough English, he might get a job in a factory. He is not happy with his newly acquired living conditions. He has difficulty comprehending the highly organized society which is sometimes guided by the utilization of technological knowledge and at other times by irrational and ruthless prejudices. Nonetheless, he suffers sorrows, affronts, mockery, and disdain with the thought that all this is transitory. After all, as soon as his economic situation improves, the time will come when he can return to the Island. When he does return, he enjoys life with gusto; that is, until his savings are spent. Then his goal once again is to accumulate enough money to board the first plane heading for New York. This cycle repeats itself over and over.[36]

What can the migrant do to remedy the ills which daily confront him? Where does he go for advice, comfort and aid? These questions will be treated in following chapters.

CHAPTER 10

Assimilation

WRITING IN 1938, CHENAULT STATED THAT MIGRATION HAD COME mainly from urban areas on the island, that it contained a slightly greater percentage of white people than found on the island, and that it included an almost equal number of males and females. He suggested that equality of numbers between sexes might be taken to indicate that the migration was almost entirely a family movement. Mills's 1948 study of the two core settlement areas in New York concurred with Chenault on the urban background of the migrants. He found that seventy percent of them came from the island's two largest cities. However, he found that the migration contained more women than men (the core areas' sex ratio being 63M/100W), that the urban migrants had more schooling and that the proportion of non-whites was higher than on the island. Abram J. Jaffee in *The Puerto Rican Population of New York City*, on the other hand, found fifty-eight percent males, more families, and more whites than Mills.[1] Frederick P. Thieme, in "A Comparison of Puerto Rican Migrants and Sedentes"[2] characterizes the migrants as lighter in color, better nourished, and better educated, on the average, than the sedentes (sedentary ones at home).

The most recent study, *Characteristics of Passengers who Travelled by Air between Puerto Rico and the U.S., 1958–1962,* shows that males predominate in the migration and that less than half of the migrants came from the largest urban centers on the island. From the studies by Chenault, Mills, Thieme, Jaffe, and the Bureau of Labor Statistics, it would appear that the selectivity of the migration has varied over the years.[3] Obviously such sociodemographic characteristics affect the Puerto Ricans' ability to assimilate.

As the migrant from *La Isla Verde* enters the United States, he hears the same rhetoric as did earlier newcomers; but whether he can follow the classic pattern of assimilation in the 1970's is an open question. By and large, islanders have come at a time when—as in the Great Depression of the 1930's—the rate of upward mobility, a key feature of the classic pattern, has been difficult. More recently Puerto Ricans enter an American class structure that has become increasingly more flexible in many respects. But the mobility of the islanders, nevertheless, according to some observers, is hampered by 1) the fact that they are occupationally restricted, 2) that by mainland standards two-thirds are colored, and thus cannot rise as easily or as far as people of white stock;[4] 3) the fact that among the migrants there is a great percentage of women.

The question of social mobility is crucial to the discussion of assimilation. Social mobility is often considered an indicator of the degree of assimilation. Social mobility, like geographic mobility, is contingent upon numerous factors: age, education, occupation-income, and color.

The Puerto Rican population is a young population. The median age for both males and females of Puerto Rican origin is approximately 21 years while the median age for all United States males is 29 and for females 30. First-generation Puerto Ricans have a median age of 28 years while the second-generation Puerto Ricans are very young with a median age of six years. The age differential between the first and second-generation Puerto Ricans reflects the recency of the group's migration and The age differential between the first- and second-generation makes comparisons between the two groups difficult.

Education is one of the most important factors working for the assimilation of the migrant into the larger community. First-generation Puerto Ricans of all ages and of both sexes have, on the average, completed fewer years of formal schooling than the second generation. Recent figures indicate an increase in the number of migrants from rural areas where opportunity for formal schooling is considerably less than in the urban centers. The median school years completed for the second generation is 10.3 year for males and 10.8 years for females. This is similar to the total distribution in the United States. Remembering what has been said previously concerning the quality of education available in areas of high Puerto Rican settlement, figures stating time spent in school hold different significance for the various groups.[5] In other words, even if Puerto Ricans remained in school long enough to compare with the national average, they would still be at a disadvantage due to a lack of up-to-date facilities and resources and the scarcity of qualified teachers and administrators. Nevertheless, the second-generation Puerto Ricans are moving up the educational ladder toward the level of the total United States population.

Occupation and employment status are "visible" signs of the role a particular ethnic group plays in the economic life of the community. Whether a large percentage of the minority group is employed or unemployed indicates its economic participation in the community and this in turn can either help or hinder the group's assimilation.

Puerto Rican men (ages 25–34) of both the first and second generation show about the same proportion in the labor force. This proportion is slightly less than the United States total. Puerto Rican men in this age group also tend to be unemployed in a greater proportion when compared with national averages, with the second generation demonstrating less unemployment than the first. Adult female Puerto Ricans exhibit approximately the same proportion (39 percent) of those employed or presently looking for work over the generations. This percentage is higher than the United States total. Unemployment among female workers, while higher than the United States total, decreases between women of the first and second generation. These data suggest that while unemployment among Puerto Ricans is higher than the national average, nevertheless, it has declined between the first and second generations. Also suggested is the idea that females appear to be more successfully integrated into the labor market than the males. The kind of work available to the Puerto Rican and his accompanying wage have undergone several changes.

The recent occupational situation shows a great proportion of first-generation men used as "operative and kindred workers." The second generation rates higher than the first in professional and craftsman categories.

Women, also, in the second generation have progressed and moved out of the "operative and kindred" categories, into a higher status, "clerical and kindred" occupations. Again, this distribution comes closer to the total United States situation than does the first generation. These data suggest that significant occupational mobility has occurred over the last generation and a moving toward United States norms.[6]

Color, perhaps the most crucial element in determining social mobility, is the most delicate factor in social mobility. It also is the most delicate factor in the social equation. Two different culturally prescribed ways of reacting to this characteristic have come into play. The more distinguishing and socioeconomically based "Latin" code has been rejected by the black and white "Anglo" color code. The tension which has resulted—especially for those of "intermediate color" and social position according to the Latin code—is well documented and does not require further elaboration. In most instances color is the steepest barrier in the assimilation process.

The Puerto Rican of today encounters a unique situation because of what many writers have called the "communications revolution" brought about especially by things that "plug into walls."[7] With radio and television the migrant of today is brought immediately into contact with the events and problems of the new culture. At one and the same time this makes his assimilation easier and yet more complex—also more challenging.

The Puerto Rican who comes to cities such as New York is also influenced by the earlier drive of other colored minorities for justice and dignity—especially the Negro. Recent Puerto

Ricans arrive in New York City, for example, at a time when approximately a million and a half black citizens have already been influenced greatly by civil rights activity and the movement for "black power."

The change in the economic area is also faster and more complex. Automation has almost created a new economy. Jobs which were once opportunities for migrants have now been eliminated by the hundreds and thousands—but this change offers new promises also: "Thus the coming of the Puerto Ricans is not just a repetition of the past, because the past no longer exists; and no people quite like the Puerto Ricans have ever come before."[8] Confronted with these new and multitudinous problems, where does the Puerto Rican migrant go? To whom does he turn?

Traditionally migrants have turned inward. They have sought strength and comfort from members of their own group, or other foreigners who like themselves feel lost, uprooted, and in need of friends. The Puerto Ricans have, perhaps more than any previous migrant group, been able to maintain ties with home. Given the large and constant number of returning migrants, one can almost say that the Puerto Rican migration has been circular in nature. The easy return to the *patria chica* (little homeland) has in some ways hindered the assimilation process. Many Puerto Rican migrants see their sojourn in the United States as akin to the "forty years in the wilderness" which will be terminated in the shortest time possible. These people do not consider assimilation a serious problem and in fact would most likely view any "Americanization" as a cultural threat. While this extreme position is not representative of the majority of newcomers, a milder form is often revealed by complaints about the difficulty in breaking into American society and by nostalgia for the better days on *la isla*.

This migration has been quite unlike that of the European who after severing his roots with the homeland by 3,000 to 4,000 miles of ocean became an "instant American." Not so the Puerto Rican. Cheap jets, lack of passport requirements as well as the cold climate and culture shock have caused many a Puerto Rican to think of packing his bag and reaching home in three hours. Even the fellow who decides to stay can dream and agree with the Puerto Rican schoolteachers who stated: "This is no place to raise kids; when I marry, back to *la isla* I go."[9]

It was on the island itself that organizations for work promotion and information purposes were first formed. As the number of migrants rose, the work of these informal organizations was assumed by the Commonwealth government in conjunction with the United States Labor and Migration departments. In the beginning, both the government of the Commonwealth of Puerto Rico as well as the United States government concentrated on predominantly "economic" goals such as placement, fair wages, safe and cheap transportation, and sanitary living conditions; however, greater emphasis has increasingly been placed on the sociocultural questions involved in the migration process.[10] The Puerto Rican government has provided constructive leadership in attacking the problems besetting the Puerto Rican migrant by promoting orientation programs, placement services, job planning and training programs as well as instruction in English.

Challenged by the rapid changes in today's society and confronting the problems of racial tension and language, the Puerto Rican migrants—huddled in cheap and squalid quarters—carried almost a guarantee to incubate rebellion as well as crime. Such hostility meant poor assimilation. As a result:

... The Puerto Rican government, appalled at the reputation the island was gaining through the misadventures of its sons and daughters in the United States, set up an indoctrination and employment office in New York, as well as a pre-departure preparation center in San Juan.[11]

The important role of the Puerto Rican Labor Department working in conjunction with the United States Employment Service has already been noted. The Department of Labor, however, sponsors other programs and activities of a wide variety which help in the orientation process.

In Puerto Rico the Labor Department carries on a special program of orientation. Its staff works through the press and radio and through schools and municipal officials in every town, to locate pilgrims before they leave Puerto Rico. They tell what job opportunities are in continental areas and where jobs and housing are scarce. By now, almost every family in Puerto Rico has relatives in some continental city and most Puerto Ricans who move to the States nowadays move because relatives have located jobs for them. The orientation staff warns people about the need for having winter clothing, tells where the Labor Department Mainland offices are in case they need help in finding health services, housing, English classes. They pass out leaflets in English and Spanish which tell about the need for having birth certificates, marriage certificates, driver's licenses, which warn against being taken in by rackets, whether they involve spurious offers of jobs, or usurious rates for installment buying.

The United States offices in turn operate employment referral services, provide similar types of information about local law and customs, and work closely with schools, churches, settlement houses, employers, labor unions, state employment services, and other government and private civic, social, welfare, and educational organizations.[12]

Since the early 1940's the Puerto Rican government has steadily supported liberal labor legislation. The Commonwealth government has been in the vanguard of those sponsoring minimum wages, paid vacations, disability insurance, and many other benefits for workers in Puerto Rico and on the mainland. The government also sponsors and implements legislation pertaining to conditions of seasonal workers. Trade unionism, therefore, has not been strong in Puerto Rico. However, union organizations have actively striven to incorporate the Puerto Rican worker via job-training programs, language classes, and bilingual publications. The Community Services Committee of the AFL-CIO directs local leadership training institutes in which Puerto Ricans have participated. Nine international unions affiliated with the AFL-CIO have headquarters in Puerto Rico. The International Ladies Garment Workers Union has had a major influence on the Spanish-speaking worker.[13] Many local unions sponsor social events, conduct business meetings in both Spanish and English, and issue materials in Spanish. The ILGWU's official publication, *Justice*, is printed in Yiddish, Spanish, and Italian. It should also be stressed that unions often have an important political function of "getting out the vote."

In continental United States, as in Puerto Rico, those early organizations dealing with Puerto Rican migrants were basically concerned with placement and labor relations; however, as the number of migrants grew and their "adjustment problems" correspondingly increased, different types of organizations and institutions appeared. This change has been reflected in the new emphasis on the United States Migration Division's activities.

Since 1949 that agency has organized a campaign in New York City to urge newcomers to take advantage of night schools, radio and television programs to improve language as well as vocational skills. Annually several hundred thousand leaflets have been utilized with the aid of teachers, priests, preachers, police and social workers to improve conditions for Puerto Ricans.[14]

The new emphasis centers on education which will facilitate the Puerto Ricans' assimilation into the larger American society and render them more attuned to the advantages of a cultural pluralism. This is the overall goal of such organizations as ASPIRA (an action agency formed under the direction of the Puerto Rican Forum and the Puerto Rican Association for Community Affairs in 1961) and the South Bronx Project. ASPIRA includes in its goals 1) motivation and orientation for capable high school students who wish to enter professional and technical fields; 2) acquisition by youths of an adequate knowledge of their cultural background to enhance their sense of self-image and identity; 3) leadership training for young people to increase the desire to face up to community problems.[15] Thus through professional consultation ASPIRA is able to help students formulate realistic educational plans.

The South Bronx Project is sponsored by the New York Public

Library. Initiated in June, 1967, and federally funded, this program under the leadership of Lillian Lopez claims three main objectives:

1) To establish and demonstrate effective library programs, methods, and materials, and to introduce the value of these services and books in nine rapidly changing neighborhoods which have become primarily Spanish-speaking.

2) To encourage the use of the library by individuals, groups, and organizations previously unaware of library services.

3) To test materials and to reassess local library collections in meeting the interests and needs of the local community.[16]

The project consists of a bilingual staff of professional and semiprofessional personnel who work as liaison between the Puerto Rican community and the New York Public Library system. Project staff members have worked with over two hundred organizations such as schools, churches, youth, as well as senior citizens' groups, to name a few. There now exist nine project branches which have some 30,000 books available in Spanish and more than 50,000 volumes in English. The staff is involved in numerous programs ranging from consumer education to cultural and historical programs dealing with the heritage of the Spanish-speaking people.

During the project's first year, more than 16,000 men, women, and children were introduced to the library through 489 programs; the second year, an intensified approach to programming brought more than 45,000 people to 990 library-sponsored events.

Approximately half the programs are held in Spanish, a quarter in a combination of Spanish and English, and the remainder in English. Community participation has been emphasized from the planning stage through the actual event.[17]

The United States Labor Department has also backed educational programs. Central to this effort are job-training programs. A 1970 Federal study conducted by Herbert Beinstock, regional director of the Bureau of Labor Statistics, had this to say about the results of such programs:

Federal labor experts are reporting signs of benefits for Puerto Ricans here in job-training programs although they remain "the most deprived of all workers" in major poverty neighborhoods. . . . The study was based largely on data for Central and East Harlem, the South Bronx and the Bedford-Stuyvesant section of Brooklyn. About 150,000 Puerto Ricans, a sixth of the city's estimated total, live in these areas. . . . Of 43,600 Puerto Ricans over 16 years of age in the poverty areas' labor force, more than an eighth—5,800—had completed a training program. Their unemployment rate was 5.2 per cent, compared with 10.3 per cent for Puerto Ricans who did not complete such training.

The 5,500 trainees with jobs averaged $2.46 an hour, compared with $2.08 for all employed Puerto Ricans in their neighborhoods. Their upgrading was indicated by a tripled proportion in skilled trades—29 per cent, compared with the over-all group's 10 per cent. In addition, 43 per cent were in white-collar work, compared with an over-all 28 per cent. The study also brought out a comparison of jobs city-wide in 1960 for 179,513 workers 14 years and older who had been born in Puerto Rico and 14,989 who were only of Puerto Rican parentage.

Mr. Bienstock cited this as showing a second-generation "moving-up," with 27 per cent of men in professional, technical, managerial, proprietor and skilled blue-collar jobs, compared with 17 per cent in the first generation. Fifty-six per cent of second-generation women were clerical and sales workers, as against a first-generation 12 per cent.[18]

The New York public school system has been slow to respond to the needs of the increasing numbers of Puerto Rican students. This has in part been due to lack of funds and properly trained personnel. However, while many ills still remain, some changes are occurring.

In areas with heavy Puerto Rican population, schools now have Spanish names and the Spanish language is used in early childhood training. Of roughly 250,000 Puerto Rican pupils in New York City, possibly one half speak little or no English. Because bilingual teachers are hard to come by, "scouts" are sent out to recruit from other areas and even Puerto Rico itself. Yet, if education is to aid in the assimilation of the Puerto Rican migrant and his children, a more dramatic change will have to occur as this quote aptly points out:

... The assimilation of the Puerto Ricans on the mainland implies better education for them and their children. Since our schools are organized to teach the average American, English-speaking student, new provisions need to be made to accommodate these Americans whose background is dissimilar to ours. Some schools are already doing this and quite successfully, too; but with their limited human and financial resources, the scope of their programs is restricted. If the plight of the Puerto Ricans is to be remedied effectively, more cooperative efforts will need to be worked out between our government and that of Puerto Rico.[19]

The valuable services of the mass media as an instrument of assimilation should be stressed. As already mentioned labor unions sponsor bilingual publications. In New York alone over a dozen newspapers written in Spanish are available. *La Prensa,* the most popular paper published in Puerto Rico, is readily available. Several Spanish-speaking radio stations are in operation, and now certain television stations, especially educational programs, are promoting programs spoken in Spanish.

The Puerto Rican migrant can, if he is so disposed, seek aid and counsel in the numerous church-sponsored programs. The majority of the Puerto Rican migrants are nominally Catholic and many are what is called "non-practicing Catholics." This is in part due to the casual religious ties on the island and the absence of a native clergy. However, the Catholic Church, through such organs as the Catholic Council for the Spanish-speaking in the Southwest, the Catholic Interracial Councils, the Spanish Catholic Action group (created in New York in 1953), and the Archbishop's Committee on the Spanish-speaking in Chicago, works to provide programs of various scope.

The National Council of Churches via its Division of Home Missions concerns itself with Mexican, Indian, and Puerto Rican farm migrants, and its Department of the Urban Church concentrates on helping urban minorities.

The Unitarian-Universalist Service Committee as well as the American Friends Service Committee are further examples of groups of religious affiliation which coordinate their efforts with other religious organizations to provide relief for the disadvantaged minority groups.

Other religious associations often considered unorthodox have had an increasing influence on the Puerto Rican migrant who finds that his old ways—even his old religious traditions—do not ameliorate the unfavorable conditions which confront him. In his search for identity he may place his faith in a revivalist or spiritualist movement.

The trauma of migration for many Puerto Ricans has been ameliorated by joining revivalist groups and also by building their own churches. A survey of 1948 showed 5 percent of New York City's 300,000 Puerto Ricans to be Pentecostal.[20] Today, with roughly one millian islanders, about one family in ten belongs to and helps support a small church. Led by their own pastors from the *barrios,* singing their hymns to the rhythm of maracas, they have in effect created a church of their own. "Espiritismo ('spiritism') is frowned upon by the church but attracts many Puerto Ricans, who feel that it does not conflict with more orthodox religious practices."[21]

One of the best accounts of a spiritualist ceremony concerns a well-known spiritualist known as Ferina as she worked her "magic" from a rather typical Puerto Rican kitchen. The proceedings include the use of strange liquids, sweet odors, urns, and burning incense as well as Christian symbols including a picture or statue of Christ and the playing of the "Ave Maria." After the proper spreading of incense throughout the room and the anointing of all guests with "Florida Water" the moment approches for "communion." After strange movements and contortions the spiritual catalyst then conveyed the message *"Buenos noches."* Apparently not a human voice, but from the spirits. Silence—for a moment—and then the guests in a low reverent whisper respond *"Buenos noches."* At the end the medium, one leg shorter than the other, moved slowly across the room:

All eyes on her, in a swaying walk that was almost a dance, her large brown eyes suddenly flashing to a face in the crowd, staring at it knowingly, and then passing on. This was Ferina, one of the most renowned of the women who "work" with the spirits of the water in Spanish Harlem.[22]

Dan Wakefield's excellent description of Puerto Rican spiritualism in New York concludes by stressing the need for such "religion." Historically, the world of the spirit—a blending of various culture traits—offered solace for the problem created by the powerful encroaching outsiders:

For both the Spanish and Americans brought to the island religions and rules that were different from and in fact officially opposed to the practice of the spirits. That practice had to go underground, and the people had to keep it and its life in secret while keeping another religious life in the shrines and churches imported by strangers.[23]

Another Spanish institution of a semi-religious nature which is still encountered among Puerto Ricans on the island and on the continent is the system of *compadrazgo* or co-parentage. Parents at the time of a child's baptism select *compadres* or godfathers and *comadres* or godmothers to act as sponsors. This institution serves both a religious and a socioeconomic function.

Despite the services provided by various social agencies and the government in health, welfare and employment, the network of *compadre* relationships still comprises an effective form of social security. This is now being expanded by further friendships beyond family and *compadre* lines. These new relationships bring in strangers and are carried out through community, factory, school and office life.

Any discussion of organs of assimilation must not fail to overlook those Federal institutions which have immediate contact with the minority group. The first contact the Puerto Rican migrant has with a Federal agency, other than those involved directly in the immigration process, is usually some representative of the Health, Education and Welfare Department. The visit of the social worker is often the first opportunity at establishing a liaison between the newcomer and his host society. Because of the position of the Puerto Rican (los que hace poco que estan aquí),[24] the next encounter with a government agency is at the Welfare Office.

One-half of all families receiving welfare are Puerto Rican. One-fourth of all Puerto Rican children in the city get some form of help and one-seventh of all islanders are on some form of public assistance.

It requires special reasons to receive public aid in New York City, the usual ones being age and disablement. Puerto Ricans make no great contribution in these categories but do make up one-half of all home-relief and one-third of aid-to-dependent children cases: "And when one reads that more than half of the home relief cases consist of six persons or more, one discovers that the special misfortune that consigns so many Puerto Ricans to the relief rolls is their large number of children."[25] Thus Federal institutions, especially those responsible for the public welfare, have a great deal of contact with the migrant and exert a definite influence on his adjustment to American society.

The Puerto Ricans have not politically come of age in the United States, although several youth movements have stirred Puerto Rican political consciousness. Puerto Ricans in New York City do not possess a good voting record. This is partially a result of misunderstanding or ignorance of voting regulations and partially because of apathy. Puerto Rican apathy results largely from neglect by established political parties.[26] The last-minute, pre-election attention given to the Puerto Rican community has usually been to secure the "Spanish vote." This flagrant campaign technique is seen most clearly on the mayoralty level. The instrument used to propagandize for the incumbents among the Puerto Ricans is the Mayor's Committee on Puerto Rican Affairs. Wakefield poses an interesting thought in regard to the lack of Puerto Rican political power when he points out the difference between the Puerto Ricans and the early immigrant groups in New York City is that Puerto Ricans have developed few or no criminal gangs of adults as did the Irish, Jews, and Italians. A happy fact for the social workers, but in the long run possibly a sad one for the progress of the Puerto Ricans.

"Many oldtime observers in the city believe this lack of an adult underworld is one of the reasons why Puerto Ricans have not yet achieved any power in politics."[27] Thus criminal gangs have not served as either a viable economic or social institution among the Puerto Rican population. Juvenile gangs are an entirely different matter. In fact, it is such gangs as the Young Lords of New York and Chicago or the Latin Kings of Chicago that have been in the vanguard of what appears to be an awakening of a Puerto Rican political consciousness and cultural pride.

Given the situation in which the Puerto Rican finds himself, one can readily understand the increasingly militant attitude in the *barrios*. Like most movements dedicated to the overthrow of the status quo, the Puerto Ricans' demand for power was initially headed by disaffected youth. Like the Black Panthers with their berets and their "power to the people" sloganeering, the Young Lords (of Chicago) until 1967 were just another Puerto Rican street gang. Today they are perhaps the most potent revolutionary Puerto Rican organization in the United States.

After their "political conversion," the YLO (Young Lords Organization) under the leadership of José (Cha Cha) Jímenez realized that the real enemy was not the Latin Kings or the Paragons or the Black Eagles (rival gangs); the real enemies were Daley's Chicago Urban Renewal, local Alderman George McCutcheon, and the United States government, whose imperial colonization policy had mangled Puerto Rico. They embarked on a program of organized revolution using political weapons of strike, boycott, sit-in, and when necessary outright confiscation. They began by negotiating peace pacts among rival gangs:

... Influenced by the Lords, the 3000-member Latin Kings, the city's largest Puerto Rican gang, have begun to organize themselves politically and have started a breakfast-for-children program. At the same time the Lords have battered constantly at West Lincoln Park to establish institutions to make them serve the poor.

In the fall of 1968 they took over the Armitage Street Methodist

Church—now the People's Church—to found their headquarters and began a day-care program.

In the spring of 1969 they led hundreds of their Puerto Rican brothers down the street to an empty lot which was to be made into $1,000-membership private tennis courts, and transformed it into a children's park.

By summer they had built a coalition with several other community organizations to fight an Urban Renewal plan that envisioned West Lincoln Park as an "inner-city suburb" for middle-income whites. That battle still wears on as the Lords and their allies have joined with architects and lawyers to present their own plans for poor people's housing.

Last winter they opened a free health clinic in the basement of the People's Church, initiating the first attack on the health problems of the entire Puerto Rican community.[28]

The Chicago Young Lords have influenced the formation of similar groups throughout the country. One such allied organization is the Young Lords of New York City. These two groups express their common development and goals in the phrase *compañeros revolucionarios* (revolutionary comrades). Nevertheless, in June of 1970 a political split occurred. The New York Young Lords became the YLP, Young Lords Party. Although the YLP has espoused similar goals to those of the YLO—focusing on the immediate needs of the people such as housing, education, health care, a difference of opinion as to organization, tactical style, and priorities has caused a schism. The composition of the two groups could also be a factor for, as Omar Lopez and Tony Baez, YLO Minister of Information and YLO Communications Deputy, respectively charge:

... The Chicago group is made up largely of high school dropouts and some who didn't finish grammar school. The New York chapter evolved out of a political organization called the Sociedad Abizu Campos, most of whose members had either graduated from or dropped out of college in or around New York. The Chicago people feel that the New Yorkers were preoccupied with ideological refinement whereas they had neither the time nor the educational background to concentrate on theoretical work.[29]

The New York group does not consider its concerns abstract. In their view, a lack of ideological clarity in Chicago was part and parcel of a number of related problems: lack of organizational discipline, leading to inconsistency in on-going programs; inadequate internal political education; frequent changes in leadership; erratic publication of the national paper—shortcomings that are to a large extent acknowledged by the Chicago group.[30]

The YLP, like the YLO, have nevertheless concentrated on community action. In July, 1969, when unable to obtain brooms from the Sanitation Department to clean 110th Street in *El Barrio,* they enlisted the aid of the neighborhood residents and constructed a garbage barricade. During the fall of 1969 they conducted clinics for welfare mothers. In October they completed a door-to-door lead poisoning detection campaign. They found high incidences of lead poisoning due to the illegal use of cheap and toxic lead paint by tenement landlords.

In an attempt to initiate a free breakfast-for-children campaign utilizing the First Spanish Methodist Church on 111th Street and Lexington Avenue, the YLP began an eleven-day occupation on December 28, 1969. They renamed the building the People's Church and succeeded in establishing "an embattled communal enclave with free breakfasts, free clothing and health services, a day-care center, a liberation school, community dinners, films, and on New Year's Eve a revolutionary service to herald 'The Decade of the People.' "[31] The influence and popularity of such organizations are without a doubt steadily increasing. However, some elements of the Puerto Rican community are alarmed by the revolutionary rhetoric and the acceptance of violence as a political tactic.

Several ad hoc groups have championed militant reformism while rejecting revolutionary tactics. One such group is La Comunidad Latin in Chicago. This citizens' organization petitioned the Chicago Board of Education for a new high school playground—and ultimately demanded a new school instead. Boston's Emergency Tenants Council sponsored a rent strike which forced one landlord to comply with city standards for safe and sanitary housing conditions. The Emergency Tenants Council's most spectacular accomplishment occurred in August, 1969, when:

> . . . the city rejected its own planner's redevelopment scheme for part of the South End in favor of one submitted by ETC. "We've never given so much responsibility to a neighborhood group," said Boston's redevelopment chief. And New York City has agreed to buy five vest-pocket parks to be built in El Barrio by East Harlem's Real Great Society.[32]

It can be said that if permitted the majority of the Puerto Rican population is willing to seek ameloriation of their problems via legally constituted organizations. In many instances the Puerto Rican migrant clings to rather conservative goals and will opt for a moderate and preferably inconspicuous manner of achieving them. According to Dr. Elena Padilla, a noted Puerto Rican anthropologist, the Puerto Rican wishes to be considered brave and doesn't want anyone to take advantage or "take you for a ride" (no dejarse coger de bobo). It is also considered wise and proper to be careful in selection of friends and to continue friendly and family relationships. Other goals as adapted to New York City include: ". . . working hard and being a 'good worker'; valuing formal education and schooling; learning English while not forgetting how to speak Spanish; cultivating the desire to 'progress' and get ahead, or 'to get the feet off the dish,' particularly through the education of one's children."[33]

Notwithstanding the basic conservatism of the migrant, a new note has been sounded by the rising political and social consciousness of American minority groups. Although the "politization" of certain Puerto Rican groups has been slow and in most instances has been a result of the influence of the Black Power movement, the revolutionary spirit which has resulted is here to stay. A new phase in minority interaction with the larger society has been initiated. Puerto Ricans are becoming aware of their place—albeit at present an often undesirable one—in American society. This in turn holds implications for further revolutionary activity as the following implies:

Most Puerto Ricans—even those impressed by the bravado and machismo of the Young Lords—support the militant reformism of the advocacy planners rather than the violence prescribed by the revolutionaries. But even the most moderate admit this could change abruptly. "We've gone through the stage of apathy, we're now at a stage of resentment—and if nothing is done to improve things dramatically we're going to be at the state of 'Burn, baby, burn,'" says Lindsay staff member Amalia Bentanzos.[34]

The Puerto Rican migrant's experience diverges from that of earlier migrants because the color prejudice and the social and economic conditions they encounter impede their freedom of movement, both in space and in social and economic status. The weakness of indigenous organization among the islanders, the lack of a native Catholic clergy and the group's very close ties with its island home, its greater dependence than earlier migrant groups on the state for services, and the Puerto Rican's cosmopolitan attitude toward color are important considerations for any understanding of the Puerto Rican migrant's acculturation. In his efforts to adjust to American society the migrant enlists the services of numerous organizations and affiliations. At present, evidence suggests that while he has slowly progressed materially, socially and culturally he has reached a dilemma. The ambiguity of his situation, and the almost insurmountable obstacles he encounters has led to the recent surge of revolutionary fervor, particularly among young Puerto Rican groups. An embryonic political consciousness mixed with cultural consciousness (and perhaps racial consciousness) has taken form and will assuredly make itself felt in the future.

CHAPTER 11

Caciquismo (Leadership)

THE PUERTO RICAN MIGRANT FACES MANY COMPLEX PROBLEMS in his efforts to adjust to American society. In the process he enlists the aid of various organizations and institutions that offer him some degree of assistance. If one were to ask, however, if the Puerto Ricans, as a collective group, are successfully coming to terms with their new environment, if they are following the classic pattern of migrant assimilation, the answer would in most cases be somewhat negative. Although Miss Maryal Knox, one of New York's prominent social workers, writes: "Her Puerto Rican neighbors are being assimilated into the life of the city faster than any previous group, partly through their own impressive efforts and partly because we (the social welfare department) are learning better how to help the process,"[1] it should be remembered that the Puerto Rican immigrant faces slum conditions and discrimination in some respects worse than any previous group.

In addition to the usual problems of the modern immigrant—automation, shifting channels of social and economic mobility, and changing racial and ethnic attitudes, his traditional value system which would have been acceptable prior to mid-twentieth century is now in conflict with current ideas. Three so-called "Latin traits" serve to distinguish the Puerto Rican from other immigrant groups. The first, *personalismo,* a belief in the innate worth and uniqueness of each man (not the equality of all men), is carried to the point of allowing someone who is more charismatic in nature to assume inordinate authority over others. At the same time, *personalismo* stresses individualism and an anti-joiner attitude. The second trait is that of *machismo.* Nar-

[144]

rowly interpreted, it refers to "he-man" ability such as sexual potency or physical courage. Innate in this belief is the fallacy that men are inherently superior to women. Family relationships among the Puerto Ricans are based upon this philosophy. Today this belief has suffered a severe shock in the face of the onslaught of Women's Liberation and the working housewife. *Humanismo* is the final cultural trait. While not actually in conflict with modern modes of living, the tradition of leaders who are poet-statesmen is for the slum dweller of New York City somewhat of an anachronism. To them, poet-governors such as Muñoz Marín and Rexford G. Tugwell have served their purpose for Puerto Rico and the Young Lord type of organizations seems more relevant to the immediate dilemmas confronting the Puerto Rican community on the continent.

Most Puerto Ricans have probably felt the need to accelerate the process of integration, the need to demonstrate their individual worth, the need to achieve self-esteem as quickly as possible. The impulse is often reflected in the number of immigrants "crashing into" the fields of sports, stage, and many of the creative arts. In these areas it is your performance and not who you are that brings success.

. . . Puerto Ricans have become prominent in several fields. There is José Ferrer of stage, screen, radio and television; Jesús María Sanromá, Boston Symphony soloist and recording artist; Admiral Horacio Rivero, U.S.N.; Graciela Rivera, opera singer; Chita Rivera, Olga San Juan, Rita Moreno, and Juano Hernández, of screen fame; Tito Puente and Noro Morales, popular orchestra leaders; and Ruth Fernández, the great interpreter of Caribbean songs. Baseball fans will recognize such former and present major league names as Vic Power, Orlando Cepeda, Ruben Gomez, Jim Rivera, Luis Arroyo, Valmy Thomas, Félix Mantilla, Arnold Portocarrero, Juan Pizarro, and Roberto Clemente. One of the top professional golfers today is Juan Rodríguez. The world's junior welterweight boxing championship was captured in 1959 by Carlos Ortiz. The bantamweight championship was held by Sixto Escobar, also from Puerto Rico, from 1934 to 1940.[2]

Looking at the experiences of various individuals who in their own right have "made it," can offer some information as to the specific ways in which these individuals have adjusted to American society.

First, in the world of sports, several outstanding Puerto Rican athletes must be mentioned. Juan A. Rodríguez Vila, more affectionately known as Chi Chi,[3] has one of the most powerful swings of any professional golfer. Born on October 23, 1935, in the Rio Piedras suburb of San Juan, Chi Chi at the age of six was a caddy at the Berwyn Country Club in San Juan. Forced to drop out of school in the eleventh grade for financial reasons, Chi Chi expressed a certain resentment when he stated: "I really like children because I was never one myself. I was too poor to be one."[4] Before deciding on a golfing career, Chi Chi tried baseball. His diminutive stature, however, ruled out any successful career as a professional.

Rodríguez's first professional tournament was the 1955 Puerto Rico Open. Within the year, financial reasons forced him to join the United States Army. During his two-year duty he sent most of his money to Puerto Rico to help support his family, but he did manage to continue his game. Upon his discharge, the Dorado Beach Hotel in Dorado, Puerto Rico, hired him to assist the noted professional golfer Ed Dudley. Under the sponsorship of Dudley, his "second father," and the cotton magnate John Weaver, Rodríguez joined the professional tour in 1960. Using women's clubs because of their lighter weight, he competed in twelve tournaments; the following year in twenty-four.

It was between the 1962 and 1963 tours that he perfected what he calls the "solid left wall principle." It is this stance that allows the physically slight, 120-pound Chi Chi to achieve the power and distance behind a 270- to 300-yard drive. The "secret" of this principle is explained in his book published in 1967 entitled *Chi Chi's Secrets of Power Golf*. This discovery led to his winning of the Professional Golfers' Association title, and the Denver Open of 1963. The following year saw him capture the Lucky International and the Western Open; however, in April, 1964, he dislocated his thumb and had to wear a protective steel sheath for more than a year. Between the years

1965 and 1967 his victories included the Dorado Pro-American and the Texas Open.[5] He played in numerous other tournaments and his winnings from 1960 through 1967 totaled $187,598.74.

He is noted for rather unorthodox behavior on the course, ranging from joking with the gallery and whistling as he walks between holes to dancing the Cha Cha around the hole after sinking a long putt; this, plus what is considered a jaunty attitude, has tended to alienate him from many of the other professional golfers while delighting his fans (known as Chi Chi's *Bandidos*).

Rodríguez explains his unorthodox behavior as a result of his desire to be liked. Troubled by the disapproval of the other golfers, Chi Chi has stated: .

It makes me want to hide in my room and do nothing but watch television and go home. It makes me miss beans and rice, which is the best thing to eat in the whole world the way my sister fixes them. ... If I can't stop bothering everybody, by being the way I am, then I'm just going to quit and go home and teach all the kids in Puerto Rico how not to be poor. That would be a good life, too.[6]

Married to the former Iwalani Lynnette Lum King, a Hawaiian of Polynesian descent, he has built a new home in Rio Piedras. When not on tour, he is head pro at Dorado Beach Hotel and is also associated with Western Airlines Golfers Club. In July of 1971, Chi Chi played an exhibition game at Coon Rapids, Minnesota, in conjunction with the Minneapolis Aquatennial summer celebrations. "Chi Chi wound up at Coon Rapids through his 14 year association with Rockresorts, Inc. which operated the Dorado Beach Hotel where he is touring pro. His affiliation with the Aquatennial derived from the Caribbean theme for the 1971 Minneapolis festival."[7]

Roberto Clemente was born in a suburb of San Juan, Carolina, August 18, 1934. He was the youngest of a large financially comfortable family. His father, who was foreman of a sugar plantation, apparently wished that Roberto might become an engineer but fate decided otherwise.

Early in his life Roberto began to display the ability and

characteristics that were to finally make him a Puerto Rican and world hero. While still in high school at age 17 he was given a $500 bonus to join the Santurce (suburb of San Juan) baseball team of the Puerto Rican League. In his third season, 1953–54, he hit at a .356 clip and the major league scouts were impressed.

After some bidding and maneuvering Clemente was acquired by the Dodgers who had won the pennant in 1953 and really couldn't play their find without the payment of a large bonus. Therefore Roberto was sent to the Montreal Club where he played part-time, batting only .257.

Apparently the Dodgers realized that they would lose Clemente in the 1954 fall draft but they had managed to keep him from their rivals, the New York Giants.

The Pittsburgh Pirates were not fooled, however. In the three previous years they had lost 317 games, finishing last each time. They needed the inspirational boost which Clemente furnished. Beginning in 1955, his eighteen seasons at Pittsburgh were phenomenal indeed.

His last hit of the 1972 season was exactly the magic number 3,000. Only ten major league players had reached this pinnacle and he was the first Latin American to do so. Clemente won four National League batting championships, played in twelve All Star Games, and was recipient of the Golden Gloves Award for spectacular fielding eleven times. Five times Clemente led the league in throwing out base runners with his powerful arm, probably the all-time best in baseball. Once from 420 feet he made a perfect throw to nip the runner trying to score at home plate. His career batting average was .317, the highest of any active player, in his last year. In 1971 he practically won the World Series from Baltimore single-handedly with his spectacular fielding and a blistering .414 average at bat. By many he was characterized as the most complete player in baseball.[8]

Opposing pitchers admitted that Clemente was great. "The big thing about Clemente," said Giant pitcher Juan Marichal, "is that he can hit any pitch. I don't mean only strikes. He can hit a ball off the ankles or off his ear." And when the great speedballer Sandy Koufax was asked for an effective way to pitch to Roberto Clemente his answer was, "Sure, roll the ball."[9]

Is it any wonder that Clemente became the great hero of the Three Rivers Stadium in Pittsburgh? When the charismatic player came to the plate the fans shouted "Arriba" (up)—meaning they wanted a ball against the wall or a home run. In the game of life as well as sports the goals of Clemente were high.

Clemente's characteristics and abilities considered in juxtaposition to the problems of minority groups seem pertinent, although somewhat difficult to analyze.

Possibly the greatest of all ball players, he was also the quirkiest. He was regarded as an extreme hypochondriac and acquired the nickname "Mr. Aches and Pains." Undoubtedly some of his ailments were real, such as pulled muscles, slipped discs, malaria, and bone chips, but he also suffered from headaches, cramps, insomnia, and from worrying about—headaches, cramps, insomnia, and his stomach. It also became axiomatic that the worse Clemente felt the better he played. As one manager put it, "If Clemente can walk, he can hit."

As Clemente gained fame and became a national hero he prided himself on possessing another trait—humbleness. He is reported as having said "I feel bashful when I get a big ovation, because I am not a big shot," adding "and I never will be."

Possibly the most significant trait of Clemente—and most pertinent for the theme of our story—is revealed after his rookie season which he finished with a modest .255 batting average. In this connection it should be remembered that Clemente was a Puerto Pican black, fiercely proud of his identity. Later in the same year he was being interviewed after a game in New York. Despite his rather modest average, his extraordinary skills were apparently very evident. The interviewer, thinking to give the 21-year-old youngster a compliment, praised his play in the day's game and series and ended by stating, "... you remind me of another [great] rookie outfielder who could run, throw, and get those clutch hits. Young fellow of ours, name of Willie Mays."[10] There was a significant silence from the Puerto Rican rookie, then "Nonetheless, I play like Roberto Clemente!" Such pride in individual and group identity was the hallmark of Clemente; it has also been the hallmark of minority group movements. This should be recognized by those who have been guilty of racial prejudice and imperialism.

In addition to his great interest in baseball, Clemente also spent much time helping others. Shortly before his death he was working on a favorite project, a "Sports City" for Puerto Rican children. Characteristically, the Pittsburgh star died (December 31, 1972) in an airplane crash just off the coast of San Juan while on a mission of mercy to aid earthquake victims at Managua, Nicaragua.

Possibly the sterling qualities of Clemente were in the minds of those who praised him when the newly elected President of Puerto Rico Rafael Hernández Colón was sworn in and declared a period of mourning for our "hero and example." Secretary of State Fernando Chardón at the outset of inaugural functions stated that "We have with us today the spirit of a man, Roberto Clemente, who helped teach *independentistas,* statehooders and commonwealthers how to play good baseball and become better citizens."[11] Mayor Lindsay of New York at the San Juan ceremony eulogized thus: "There are many things that bind the eight million people of New York and the people of Puerto Rico. . . . None . . . are more outstanding today than the grief felt over the loss of Roberto Clemente, an outstanding baseball player and humanitarian."

Roberto Clemente was enshrined in the Baseball Hall of Fame in 1973. The usual waiting period was waived and Roberto Clemente was voted into the Baseball Hall of Fame—few have achieved this honor.[12] If there was a humanitarian Hall of Fame, he would achieve that honor also.

Orlando Manuel Cepeda, born on September 17, 1937, in Ponce, Puerto Rico, whose nickname Cha Cha is similar to that of his fellow countryman Chi Chi, has also achieved fame in the area of baseball.

In his youth Orlando was called "Peruchin'" or "Little Pedro" in order to distinguish him from his famous baseball-star father. Following in his father's footsteps, the seventeen-year-old Orlando under the management of Pedrin Zorilla (after a knee operation left him on crutches for five months), joined in 1955 the Giants' minor-league training base in Melbourne, Florida, for a tryout. He was assigned to the Salem (Virginia) team in the Class D Appalachian League. The year was not a happy one. His father's death, difficulties with English and the added stigma of southern racism, caused him to request a transfer. The following years saw him play third base in the Mississippi-Ohio Valley League (Kokomo, Indiana), the Class C Northern League (St. Cloud, Minnesota), and the Class AAA American Association (Minneapolis).

It was in 1958 that his real career began. President Horace Stoneham of the Giants chose Cepeda for his first baseman. With the transfer of the Giants from New York to San Francisco, Cepeda, rather than the celebrated Willie Mays, became the fans' favorite. However, in a heated game during the Puerto Rican League play-off in 1958–1959, Cepeda lost his popularity due to a demonstration of unsportsmanlike conduct. Fans quickly change their allegiance and Cepeda regained favor following his initial 1959 slump. During mid-season, Cepeda was moved unsuccessfully to third base and then to left field to make room for a new rookie, Willie Lee McCovey.

The six-feet-two-inch-tall, 210-pound Cepeda, also nicknamed the "Baby Bull" because of his size, was married in 1960 to Ana Hilda Pino Valazquez of Puerto Rico.

From 1960 through 1964, Cepeda was among the leading batters of the National League. In both 1961 and 1962 the *Sporting News* National League All-Star team designated him first baseman. But these years were tempestuous ones for Cepeda and the Giants' management. In the first place his annual spring holdout for a raise was resented. Second, his knee injury in the 1961 season was bothering him again:

. . . The knee hurt me all the time. But . . . Dark [Alvin Dark, manager of the Giants since 1961] thought I was trying not to play. He treated me like a child. I am a human being, whether I am blue or black or white, or green. We Latins are different, but we are still human beings. Dark did not respect our differences.[13]

In December, 1964, an operation on his damaged knee resulted in his disability during most of the 1965 season. When relations improved a little under the new management of Herman Franks, Cepeda asked to be traded and was sent to the Saint Louis Cardinals on May 8, 1966.

Cepeda was warmly welcomed by the Cardinal team. He responded by finishing the 1966 season with 73 runs batted in, 20 home runs, and a .301 batting average. The Associated Press poll of baseball writers in 1966 named Cepeda as the National League's Comeback Player of the Year. In 1967 Cepeda was unanimously chosen by a panel of baseball writers as the National League's Most Valuable Player of the Year. In the same year, *Sporting News* named Cepeda the National League's Player of the Year, and again chose him as first baseman on its National League All-Star team. Because of Cepeda's Latin influence, the Saint Louis Cardinals are often called "El Birdos" [sic] in *Spanglish*.[14]

During the 1969–1970 season Cepeda was given in trade to the Atlanta Braves. However, Cepeda has been having trouble, as a recent article in the *Minneapolis Tribune* indicates:

"I don't want to be a pinch hitter," Cepeda . . . said . . . when told that the Braves' vice-president, Paul Richards, would rather Cepeda not undergo surgery on an injured left knee now so that the former regular could be available as a pinch hitter. "If I can't play every day, I don't want to play, I want to earn money," said Cepeda. "I will do everything I can to get my knee well . . . I will do anything they say."[15]

A second general category which has seen the rise of Puerto Rican talent within its ranks is the acting profession. Two outstanding examples are those of José Vicente Ferrer and the lovely Chita Rivera.

José Ferrer, actor, director, and producer, was born January 8, 1912, in Santurce, Puerto Rico. Although he graduated from Princeton in 1933 with an A.B. degree in architecture, José Ferrer has had an interesting and varied career in the world of show business.

He first appeared at the Periwinkle, Long Island, Showboat in 1934 while serving as Assistant State Manager of the Summer Theatre Stock Company, New York. The year 1935 marks his first appearance on the New York stage in *A Slight Case of Murder*. He played minor roles in numerous plays from 1936 to 1939. In 1940 he acted his first star role as Lord Fancourt Babberley in *Charley's Aunt*.

He produced, or directed and occasionally acted in such outstanding plays during the years 1950–1964 as *Stalag 17* (1951–producer-director); *The Fourposter* (1951-producer-director); *The Chase* (1952-which he directed and in which he also appeared); *Edwin Booth* (1959-which he produced and in which he played the title role); the Broadway hit *The Girl Who Came to Supper* (1963–1964-in which he starred). His films include *Joan of Arc* (1947); *Cyrano de Bergerac* (1950—title role); *Moulin Rouge* (1952); *Miss Sadie Thompson* [Rain] and *The Caine Mutiny* (1953); *I Accuse* and *The Shrike* (1958); *Return to Peyton Place* (1962); *State Fair* (1963); *Nine Hours to Rama* and *Lawrence of Arabia* (1963); *The Greatest Story Ever Told* (1964).

José Ferrer holds honors degrees and various awards for acting since 1944 which include the American Academy Award (1950), and the Academy Award (1950—best actor for *Cyrano*).

Born in Washington, D.C., on January 23, 1933, of Puerto Rican parents, the well-known Chita Rivera was originally named Concita del Rivera. She was educated at William Howard Taft High School, New York, and later married Anthony Mordente. Trained as a dancer at the American School of Ballet, she made her debut at the Imperial Theatre, New York, 1952, in *Call Me Madam*. She has subsequently performed in *46th Street* in 1953, in the chorus of *Guys and Dolls* in 1954, in *Can Can,* at the President Theatre in February, 1955, in *Shoestring Revue.* She has also played in *Seventh Heaven* in 1955; on Broadway in 1956 in *Mr. Wonderful*; as a stand-in in the Broadway play *Shinbone Alley*; in *West Side Story* as Anita in 1957; and in 1960 at the Martin Beck Theatre in New York she played in *Bye Bye Birdie.* After touring the United States and England in both *West Side Story* and *Bye Bye Birdie,* Chita in 1963 played in *Zenda* and in 1964 in *Bajour.* First appearing on television in 1956, she has since made numerous appearances. Her favorite parts are Anita in *West Side Story* and Rose Grant in *Bye Bye Birdie.*

The third and final category includes educators, statesmen, and public administrators. In addition to the interesting individuals treated previously in Part II, many others could be mentioned.

The President of the University of Puerto Rico—Rio Piedras, Jaime Benítez has had a long career as humanitarian and educator. Born in Vieques, Puerto Rico, October 29, 1908, he has received an L.L.B. from Georgetown University, 1930; L.L.M. (Honoris Causa) from Polytechnic Institute, San Germán, Puerto Rico, in 1950; L.L.D. at New York University, 1960; L.L.D. from Fairleigh-Dickinson University, 1961; L.L.D from Catholic University of Puerto Rico, 1965. He was married to Luz Martínez of Puerto Rico, August, 1941. Dr. Benitez's experience has been varied. He has served as instructor of Social Science at the University of Puerto Rico, 1941–1942; Chancellor of the University of Puerto Rico 1942–1966, President of the same from 1966 to the fall of 1971.[16]

In addition to his work at the University of Puerto Rico he has held such honorable positions as United States delegate to the Conference of Universities, Utrecht, Holland, 1948; member of the United States national committee on UNESCO, 1950–1955; member of the executive committee of UNESCO, 1951–1955; United States delegate to the UNESCO conferences at

Havana, 1950 and Paris, 1951; Presidential Commission of the Bill of Rights, Puerto Rican Constitutional Convention, 1951; recipient of the Carnegie Traveling Grant, June, 1954; as well as other noteworthy titles and honors.

He is the author of the following works: *The Concept of the Family in Roman and Common Law Jurisprudence*, 1931; *Political and Philosophical Theories of José Ortega y Gasset*, 1931; *Reflexiones Sobre el Presente*, 1950; *La Iniciación Universitaria y las Ciencias Sociales*, 1950; *Junto a la Torre*, 1963; *La Universidad del Futuro*, 1964; *Discurso en Salamanca*, 1965; *Sobre el Futuro Political y Cultural de Puerto Rico*, 1965.

Pharmacist, economist, ambassador-statesman, José Teodoro (Teddy) Moscoso was born on November 26, 1910, in Barcelona, Spain. His family home, however, was in Ponce where his father had been in the pharmaceutical business since 1898. Graduating from Ponce High School in 1928, he entered the Philadelphia College of Pharmacy and Science and later the University of Michigan where he graduated with a B.S. degree in 1932.

Returning to Puerto Rico he served as general manager of the Moscoso Hno. and Co., Inc., from 1932 to 1939. During this period his interest in low-income housing led to his membership in the municipal housing authority in Ponce of which he shortly became vice-chairman. Under the administration of Governor Rexford G. Tugwell, he was appointed housing administrator for all of Puerto Rico. As executive director, Moscoso supervised the building of five huge housing projects for slum dwellers and in 1942 was named president of the recently created Puerto Rican Industrial Development Company (*Fomento*). Teodoro Moscoso sponsored the construction of the island's first luxury hotel, the Caribe Hilton, (known as "Moscoso's folly") to stimulate the tourist trade. When the Commonwealth government set up its Economic Development Administration in 1950, Moscoso was chosen as chief administrator. Thus Teodoro Moscoso had served as one of the chief supporters and administrators of Puerto

Rico's successful development program, "Operation Bootstrap" or *Fomento*.

In March, 1961, President John F. Kennedy appointed Moscoso Ambassador to Venezuela, the first distinction of this type bestowed on a Puerto Rican. In less than a year, President Kennedy again chose Moscoso to assume an office of distinction—the duties of United States Co-ordinator of the Alliance for Progress and assistant administrator for Latin America in the Agency for International Development. Here he made his greatest contributions, for it was in his capacity as United States Director of the Alliance for Progress that his gifts in the field of statesmanship were fully appreciated. Nowhere are his views concerning the goals of the Alliance for Progress more clearly stated than in his address before the National Press Club in Washington, D.C., on February 15, 1962: "If the *Alianza* is left entirely to the economists, the technicians, and the government officials, it cannot fully succeed. For we are dealing with human emotions and aspirations, not just economic charts, bricks and machinery."[17] June, 1963, saw Moscoso appointed by President Kennedy as United States representative on the Inter-American Economic and Social Council of the Organization of American States (OAS).

Teodoro Moscoso has published a number of articles for popular magazines and newspapers. He was awarded honorary L.L.D. degrees by Fordham University, the University of Notre Dame, and the University of Michigan. He was president of the Pharmacists' Association of Puerto Rico, and of the Puerto Rican Chapter of the American Society for Public Administration in 1952. Serving as director of the Puerto Rican Urban Renewal and Housing Corporation, the Government Development Bank, and the Land Authority of Puerto Rico, he still has found time to enjoy club membership in the Bankers, the Hermitage, and Casino de Puerto Rico Clubs, and his fraternities.

Teodoro Moscocso has been a member of the Presidential Commission and the Municipal Assembly of San Juan and has worked feverishly to achieve some of the goals underlying his philosophy of a "peaceful revolution for Latin America."

Herman Badillo, born in Caguas, Puerto Rico, in 1929, is the first person of Puerto Rican birth to become a member of the Congress of the United States. Badillo, elected on November 3, 1970, received 85 percent of the votes cast in New York's 21st Congressional District. He came to New York City as an orphan in 1940, and was educated in the public schools and colleges of New York, supporting himself in a variety of jobs ranging from setting up pins in a bowling alley to working as a short-order cook.

In 1951, Badillo graduated *magna cum laude* from the City College of New York as a Bachelor of Business Administration, having majored in accounting and economics. In 1954, he graduated *cum laude* from Brooklyn Law School. In 1956, he became a Certified Public Accountant.

In 1960, Badillo set up the John F. Kennedy Democratic Club in East Harlem and in 1962, Mayor Wagner appointed him Commissioner of the newly-created Department of Relocation; at 33, Badillo was the youngest Commissioner in the City Administration. Described as a slender man with a shock of dark hair, dark blue eyes, he is very tall, so tall that the *New York Post* in 1970 declared him to be "tall enough to see beyond the Bronx."

Badillo achieved victory in the Democratic primary for Bronx Borough President in 1965 and went on to win the general election in the fall. In that office, Badillo brought more capital construction funds into the Bronx than any other Borough President in the City's history. In 1968 Badillo was Delegate to the 1968 Democratic National Convention and represented New York on the Credentials Committee.

He did not seek reelection in the Bronx; in 1969 he chose instead to enter the Democratic mayoral primary. He finished a strong third in the race. He was elected to Congress in 1970. Mr. Badillo has practiced law with the firm of Stroock & Stroock

& Lavan, served as Chairman of the Task Force on Election Reform, and was a member of New York City's Hospitals Corporation. He is a member of the House Education and Labor Committee; General Subcommittee on Education; Special Subcommittee on Labor; Subcommittee on Agricultural Labor; Special Poverty Oversight Subcommittee.

Herman Badillo has long been an ardent champion of social justice for all Puerto Ricans as the following quote from a speech of May 4, 1971, in the United States House of Representatives indicates:

Mr. Speaker, because of my place of birth and background I feel a special responsibility for Puerto Rico and Puerto Ricans, whether they be in the South Bronx; in Lorain, Ohio; or in Caguas, where I was born. If we are going to meaningfully and effectively cope with our urban crisis and the impending influx of Puerto Rican migrants, we must make certain Puerto Rico receives its full and fair share and that the island's economic development and progress is encouraged and aided to the fullest extent possible. I urge our colleagues to actively participate in this vital undertaking and to work with me in ending the current discrimination against Puerto Rico and in bringing equity to the treatment of "La Isla Verde" as well as to the more than one million Puerto Ricans now on the mainland.[18]

One of the most colorful Puerto Rican political figures is the recently retired woman mayor of San Juan, Felisa Rincón de Gautier. Doña Fela, as she is affectionately known, has been described as:

. . . a distinguished-looking woman, with aquiline features and blue-grey hair that she augments with a switch and stacks in handsome coiled braids atop her head, sometimes backing these up with a splash of white feathers. She dresses smartly and has a twinkle in her eye.[19]

Born in 1897, she has had a long and active political career which is extraordinary for a woman in a Latin culture. Entering politics in the 1930's as a member of the Liberal Party, she became one of the founders of the PPD (Partido Popular Democrático) in 1938. Since 1940 she has been chairwoman of the

San Juan committee of the party and since 1946 Mayor of San Juan.

Doña Felisa has acquired a political style all her own. Widely known throughout the Americas due to her extensive travels, she is also noted for her charity work among the urban poor. On one of her frequent campaign trips to New York, where she speaks on behalf of the Democratic candidates among New York Puerto Ricans, she might be observed among a group that could include dozens of Negroes, Puerto Ricans, and Jewish politicians —sometimes possibly a governor. The program offers speeches of course, and sometimes rock-and-roll with zany acts but:

... During these events Doña Felisa registered surprise at times, but always poise and good humor too. And she made a speech herself, in nearly perfect English, in the course of which she urged her country-men who were present to "do everything you possibly can for the good name of Puerto Rico."[20]

In Puerto Rico Felisa Rincón de Gautier is the astute politician that her longevity in office would imply. Coupled with this political astuteness is a certain flair and manner which until the last few years has kept her San Juan political machine firmly under her control.

During her long period at City Hall she was observed as an elegant figure always poised with her turbans, Spanish fans and rather queenly manner. She might fly a plane-load of snow down from New York for Spanish waifs to enjoy or use public funds to spread toys, candy, and other gifts among the poor.

... When a slum dweller from *La Perla* needed roofing materials for his seaside shack, he saw Doña Fela, who gave him a *papelito*. . . . This problem-solving apparatus was politically prudent and humane, but, later, hardly up to the scale of San Juan, a city that could no longer be fixed with *papelitos*.[21]

Criticism of her practices has resulted and the PPD made poor showings in the 1964 election and the 1967 plebiscite in San Juan. In 1968 she retired as Mayor of San Juan.

Part IV

Retrospect and Prospects

Retrospect and Prospects

HE WHO IS DARING ENOUGH MIGHT PREDICT THE FUTURE TURN OF events in Puerto Rico. Such a writer would have to be bold indeed and might well utilize both necromancy and the crystal ball.

The people and the problems of the island are difficult to analyze. Some fanatical Nationalists in 1950 attempted to assassinate Governor Muñoz Marín and his family at La Fortaleza as well as President Truman at Blair House in Washington, D.C. At the same time, voluntary enlistments in the Korean War by loyal patriots set a record for all states of the union.

These are people who are, as a rule, not called Americans by their fellow citizens on the continent and are rarely thought of as Latin Americans by their blood cousins of *Tierra Firme*.

Moreover, many now seem disenchanted with the concept *Estado Libre Asociado* and seem ready to withdraw support from the program carried out under the aegis of Operation Bootstrap, a program which has been grandiose in its conception, operation, and results.

Because of his success in the 1940 election and subsequent developments, Muñoz Marín with the aid of Tugwell and others achieved the Elective Governor Act (Crawford-Butler Act) which was signed by President Truman on August 4, 1947. The *Populares* were successful in the 1948 election and Muñoz Marín became the first elected governor of the island and served four terms until he withdrew in favor of his hand-picked successor, Roberto Sanchez Vilella, in 1964.

Muñoz himself received more honors than most men in public life. He was granted numerous decorations and at least four universities, including Harvard, granted him the degree of

[163]

Doctor of Laws. He was among the first to receive the Presidential Medal of Freedom.

As a result of the overall achievements of Puerto Rico during these years, the island became a symbol of self-help and success for many underdeveloped areas of the world.

The special visits made to Puerto Rico for academic and social reasons have proved to be of great significance. Since 1952 over 9,000 visitors representing more than 130 countries have come to the island to view the accomplishments in the various areas of social progress.[1] Puerto Rico's relationship with the United States has changed indeed from what it was in the colonial period.

A study of Puerto Rico reveals that its society is *sui generis* a mixture of many elements. The same could be said for its *la lucha* (struggle) for a better life. But despite the unique nature of the Puerto Rican revolutionary change (and possibly because of it), the sociopolitical horizon appears very troubled for *la isla verde.*

Maybe this should not be shocking inasmuch as various segments of society throughout the world have suffered from identity crises—students, women, and especially previously exploited minorities, including blacks, Chicanos, and Puerto Ricans. Undoubtedly this explains the extremism of the *independentista* element in Puerto Rico, as we have already indicated. But it is also present among Puerto Ricans in continental United States and expresses itself in various ways. It is not always associated with the drive for independence for the island but is definitely linked with the dignity and worth of the individual. The personal problem seems to be the dilemma of Piri Thomas as he philosophizes with Brew about their mutual friend Gerald as well as his reaction to joining the "true" religion of Islam:

"What yuh mean 'like you an' me'?" he said.

"You and me," I said. "You hate Gerald's guts because he don't wanna be a spook and you hate whites for the reason known to a whole certain race that you happen to be part of. And I feel the same because I'm hung up. I still can't help feeling both paddy and Negro. The weight feels even on both sides even if both sides wanna feel uneven. Goddammit, I wish I could be like one of those lizards that change colors. When I'd be with Negroes, I'd be a stone Negro, and with paddies, I'd be stone paddy. It ain't like that with Gerald. He got used to his choice even before he had made it, so it's all over for him inside. It ain't like that with me. Mine is startin' for real an' I'm scared of this hate with one name that's chewing me up. So dig it, Brew, if I'm talking one way one time and another way another time, it's only 'cause I wanna know, 'cause I ain't been born but this one time. Understand?"²

I learned many things, because it involved me. I became curious about everything human. Though I didn't remain a Muslim after my eventual release from the big jail, I never forgot one thing that Muhammad said, for I believed it too: "No matter a man's color or race, he has a need of dignity and he'll go anywhere, become anything, or do anything to get it—anything . . ."³

Recent articles dealing with the YLO (Young Lords Organization) of Chicago and the YLP (Young Lords Party) of New York indicate that these Puerto Rican groups which could once be rated as vandalistic street gangs are now becoming a rather potent force for revolutionary change. It is especially significant that much of their activity might be described under the heading of general welfare which is mentioned several places in the Constitution of the United States.⁴ In Chicago, for example, their projects have resulted in improved children's parks, free health clinics and better housing; much the same can be said for the New York group. In fact, the slogan of a recent YLP parade in *El Barrio* was "Despierta Boriqua. Defiende lo tuyo." "Awake, Puerto Rican. Defend what is yours." And when asked by a reporter how they could continue to take over property for general welfare purposes the answer was, "Because we serve our people. That's why we could move from People's Church to a T. B. truck to Lincoln Hospital—and you-all don't know where we're gonna be tomorrow."⁵ It is significant that these radicals are concerned with serving Puerto Ricans in the United States. In other words, meeting the identity crisis does not have to be equated with independence for Puerto Rico or the political status issue.

On the other hand, no single issue stirs Puerto Rican emotions as much as the status issue and a definitive settlement is long overdue. To some Puerto Ricans, undoubtedly, the political independence of the island is related to a very personal feeling of pride. Muñoz Marín undoubtedly favored independence as a member of the Liberal Party in the 1930's. In his drive for political control and social justice, however, he was able to postpone and minimize the status issue. The very fact that he was able to dominate the political scene so long indicates how successful his drive for a decent life for the people turned out to be.

Muñoz always maintained, however, that Public Law 600 which granted Commonwealth status was worked out in the nature of a contract or compact and was not subject to unilateral modification or change by Congress. This is brought out in his Godkin Lectures delivered at Harvard in 1959. Therein he pointed out that the compact idea removed the onus of colonialism from the United States-Puerto Rico relationship. He also stressed the point that a rich cultural pluralism could take place in love of *patria* without people demanding what he characterized as a "narrow or petty concept of the national state." He also implied in these lectures that in view of the "absolute power of nuclear weapons" complete national independence for both small and large nations might become a shibboleth. To drive home his points he quoted Dr. Fernós Isern who, as acting delegate of the United States and Resident Commissioner of Puerto Rico, was an extraordinary symbol of the unity of purpose and understanding needed for United States-Puerto Rico relationships.

Contrary to the position taken by the Independence Party, as well as that held by the Nationalist and Communist groups, the people of Puerto Rico hold that the Constitution and the laws of the Commonwealth can be amended, suspended or repealed only by their authority and that the compact between the United States and Puerto Rico can only be amended or repealed by mutual consent. . . . This is also the understanding of the United States of America.[6]

The very title of Muñoz Marín's lectures "Breakthrough from Nationalism," is significant. His was the poet's dream of a people everywhere free from want and poverty and capable of world brotherhood, proud of their own culture, but also respectful of their neighbors.

Unfortunately, Congress did not espouse the compact idea and modification of the Commonwealth status in accordance with the wishes of Muñoz Marín. In ratifying the agreement which led to the *Estado Libre Asociado* of 1952, Congress had made it clear that the island was still subject to the Federal Relations Statute which outlined areas of Congressional jurisdiction. The attitude of the U.S. legislature might be compared to that of the British Parliament in 1775; the legislators failed to consider the future and the Puerto Rican point of view. Thus the island was really subject to the oligarchic rule of the American Congress, a rather large body representing especially the interests of the continental United States.

Gradually it became clear to some Puerto Rican leaders that the imperfect Commonwealth creation of Muñoz Marín represented his permanent policy. As a result some associates became statehood supporters, others *independentistas*.

Finally, in 1963, after some 66 years of association with Puerto Rico, Congress set up a 13-man Commission to study and report on the island's political status. The issue is still entangled with contradictions and complexities. In 1967, however, a plebiscite was held in Puerto Rico on the status issue; the Commonwealth idea won 66.5 percent of the votes compared with 38.9 percent for statehood and less than 1 percent for independence. However, the referendum was boycotted by extreme nationalists.

Philosophers and statesmen throughout the ages have stressed the need for a state organization, and this necessitates the surrender of certain elements of freedom in order for everyone to avoid anarchy. Lenin has stated, "While the state exists there is no freedom. When there is freedom, there will be no state."[7] Inasmuch as the extremists' strategy in Puerto Rico approximates anarchy, the seminal issue then is what form of autonomy seems most appropriate for the future—statehood, independence, commonwealth, or a modified commonwealth.

At an early stage one of the great Puerto Rican heroes, Don Luis Muñoz Rivera, clearly saw that meaningful autonomy was absolutely necessary for the island. Apparently he had some doubts about the acquiring of United States citizenship for Puerto Ricans, but after returning from a trip to the mainland in September of 1899 he wrote as follows:

I come from a country whose vigor is the wonder of the world. . . . Beholding the moral and physical power of that race, I, sirs, never felt envy: I felt the stimulus to reach those heights . . . through the arts of labor and through civic commitment. We must move rapidly toward identity . . . and ask for Puerto Rico to be transformed into a kind of California or Nebraska, with our own initiatives, with our own laws, with our own practices, equal in duty and rights; equal in advantages, equal, if there are sacrifices, in sacrificing. Inequality is inferiority. And we reject it as proudly, as frankly and as resolutely as New York or Pennsylvania might reject the harshnesses and abuses of dictatorship.[8]

Since the new Progressive Party and Luis A. Ferré won the governorship in 1968 advocating statehood, that ideology has become more popular. Graffiti scrawled about downtown San Juan and other cities proclaim: *estado 51* (state number 51). Apparently this trend has gained momentum because of statehood achieved by Hawaii and Alaska. It is also significant that Puerto Rican migrants writing from New York, Chicago, Philadelphia, Milwaukee, Boston, etc., to friends and families back home speak of themselves as second-class citizens and that only statehood will give them equality in America.[9]

Since the 1952 election the percentage favoring statehood has increased from about 13 percent to 45 percent. It should be noted, however, that the combined vote of the two parties (Popular Democratic and Peoples) advocating some form of commonwealth status exceeds (almost 52 percent) the statehood vote (45 percent).[10]

Inasmuch as the crisis of identity is associated with social justice as well as with some form of "state" sovereignty, the continental situation should be considered. Throughout the past century the general-welfare aspect of good government deriving from the United States Constitution has come largely because of Federal action rather than from a "Barry Goldwater states-rights type of ideology." In other words, migrant blacks, Puerto Ricans, or Chicanos could expect little social justice in the past from such states at Alabama, Texas, or California. Regarding this issue Milton Mayer contends that "We are witnessing in our time, in the civil rights struggle . . . the slow death throes of the states-rights type of ideology, exemplified by such commonplace newspaper headlines as: 'U.S. Threatens Aid Cutoff to Alabama.' "[11]

The pertinent question which the Puerto Rican *jíbaro* of the mountains, the tenant in *El Fanguito,* or the migrant worker in the United States must ask is: Will the rather conservative statehood group with men like Ferré as leaders bring more freedom, combined with social justice? It is also pertinent to stress that the problem of the Puerto Rican *jíbaro* is similar to that of migrant workers of New York, New Jersey, Michigan, etc.

In a recent article Governor Ferré has set 1980 as a target date for the achievement of statehood. There might, however, be considerable opposition from the "Bible Belt" area to admission of a predominantly Catholic Puerto Rico as well as to a region rated as largely black. Some observers, therefore, maintain that statehood will only be achieved—if at all—in the distant future. In the meantime, the identity crisis demands significant change!

Possibly the ideology most difficult to evaluate is the desire for a complete break from the United States, advocated by such parties as the Liberals, Nationalists, and the *independentistas.* On record the percentage favoring this status has always been small, the highest being 19 percent in the 1952 election. Recently this has dropped to only about 3 percent, but it should be noted that there is a difference between electoral strength and social power. Violence has been associated with this political segment and this, of course, harms one of the island's most lucrative activities—tourism. *Time* estimated in May of 1971 that one million visitors spent 230 million dollars on the island in 1968.

The extremists should also consider the costs and losses which might result from a complete break from continental United States. Those who criticize Puerto Rican colonialism point out that Federal agencies now control customs, immigration, the post office system, radio, television, social security, currency, and defense. Moreover, the Pentagon has numerous air and atomic bases on the island. Complete independence would give Puerto Rico control over all these, but it would also bring financial responsibility as well.

Possibly independence would bring the greatest injury to sugar production and other business activities. Sugar has been a dying industry during the last twenty years and the present government is trying to restore production by helping farmers mechanize. "But what remains of the Puerto Rican sugar industry could not survive unless it had the assurance of the stability of U.S. prices."[12] The Resident Commissioner contends that the Puerto Rican overall economy is "even more dependent now on the United States market than it was in the days when sugar was far and away the principal product of the island." It is a moot question indeed whether high-priced Puerto Rican sugar could survive without the United States market protected by a high tariff. Moreover, could business continue to prosper if the tax incentives disappeared with a change of government?

The present governor, while admitting the existence of such problems as high unemployment as late as the summer of 1971, also stresses many positive developments.

The facts about Puerto Rico compiled by nongovernment agencies show that while there are problems in Puerto Rico, progress in furthering the individual economically and culturally has been massive over these last decades. Unemployment is presently at 10.8 percent according to the Banco Popular, the island's No. 1 bank. The government of Puerto Rico is spending 32 percent of the budget for education and

$3 billion for housing over the next four years and is constantly striving to better the lot of the whole of the population. One hundred-ten new plants have been opened in the last 10 months, creating 3,963 jobs. The growth rate has been in real GNP terms, 6.5 percent in the first quarter of this year, based on annual levels.

Our gross national product for the first quarter of 1971, according to the same Banco Popular compilation, was $1.285 billion, a rise of 12.2 percent over the same quarter in 1970. The net per-capita income reached $1,426—almost 10 percent over the previous year and highest in Central and Latin America.[13]

Progress notwithstanding, the desire for some form of real sovereignty for the island is strong, emotional, and general. Most Puerto Ricans apparently are not so much against the Federal government as for accomplishing something significant for themselves. Obviously this has been encouraged by the recently achieved autonomy of such countries as Guyana, Jamaica, and Trinidad-Tobago, as well as by the Cuban revolution. On the other hand, the practical and viable nature of complete independence for many of the small countries is open to question. From the standpoint of freedom and social justice, the value of so-called "independence" for some older countries might even be questioned—Haiti, for example.

Perhaps Muñoz Marín was right when he pointed out that an age which has spawned both nuclear power and worldwide economic problems should also bring on the demise or modification of present day nationalism. But there is always a feeling of nostalgia for the old and "sacred." The feudal days of the Round Table apparently evoked emotional support also. According to Alfred Lord Tennyson, it took three trips to the lakeshore by the bold Sir Bedivere before he could rid himself of jeweled Excalibur, the symbol of King Arthur's power and the glorious days when "all day long the noise of battle rolled among the mountains by the winter sea."

Much has been written by way of criticism about "Puerto Rico: Our Backward Colony." The designation "Happy Commonwealth" is apparently tourism rhetoric, for the island is still "blessed" with terrible slums, high unemployment, and low wages. Impoverished workers chop sugar cane in this tropical "paradise" while tax-free companies ship the raw product to the States. It is then returned, a finish product, and purchased at exorbitant prices.[14]

As recorded in the *Congressional Record*, Herman Badillo echoes much the same dismal story. Puerto Ricans are not receiving their just share of welfare payments. Primary industries, tourism, and textiles are suffering, unemployment is very high, and average wages are very low, $1.60 per hour, less than half the United States rate.[15]

However, if one peruses the charts provided by the Puerto Rican Office of the Commonwealth, the progress that has transpired since the 1940's is amazing indeed. Of course, the selected indicators chosen from this source might be the result of prejudice, but other sources substantiate this claim. An article in *Current History* (1966), for example, lists seven indicators (gross product, per capita income, motor vehicles, telephones, literacy, death rate per 1,000, as well as birth rate) which show the same sort of progress.[16] This evidence is corroborated by John R. Howard in *Awakening Minorities*, 1970 as well as by Kal Wagenheim in *Puerto Rico: A Profile,* 1970. It is probably best summarized by Thomas Aitkin, Jr., in *Poet in the Fortress,* 1964:

The statistics were appearing in scores of studies and reports. In twenty years production had risen three times in constant dollars; personal income had tripled; family income had quadrupled. The changing ownership of wealth in ten years had reduced the percentage of families earning less than $1,000 a year from 46 to 23.9, more than doubled the percentage of families whose earnings were bracketed between $2,000 and $5,000, with an even greater increase in those earning from $5,000 to $10,000. Earners over the $10,000 figure had tripled as a percentage of the population. Wages had increased from an hourly average of 19 cents in manufacturing to a level of 89 cents, in agriculture from 15 to 48 cents, and in the construction industries from 22 to 81 cents. The diet of the people had changed: the consumption of dairy products had nearly tripled, was nearly double for meat, and had more than doubled for eggs.

The island's birth rate, one of the highest in the world, had begun to decline—from 39 per thousand to 31.5—and the average life expectancy had risen from 46 years to an amazing 71.

Probably the paranoiac patriots of both political extremes and in the United States Congress and Puerto Rico should be reminded that two statesman-poets, one an "American" and one a "Puerto Rican," inaugurated revolutionary changes in the 1940's that resulted in the remarkable progress indicated above. They should also be reminded of what Chief Justice Warren stated in 1956 and Muñoz Marín echoed later:

... our American system is not static. ... It is an organism intended to grow. ... Ours is an experiment—the newest experiment and perhaps the most notable of American ... experiments in our lifetime.

La Lucha (struggle) for social-political reform, like the task of Sisyphus, is apparently never-ending.

Notes and References

Chapter One

1. The Act of May 17, 1932, 47 Stat. 158, changed the name of Porto Rico to Puerto Rico.
2. Muñoz Marín, Luis. "The Sad Case of Puerto Rico," *The American Mercury*. Feb., 1929, pp. 136–41.
3. Operation Bootstrap will be treated in detail in Part II, Chapter 3.
4. Name given to the islanders by the early Spanish explorers.
5. Of course, all people of the western hemisphere could be classed as Americans. Historically the term has been applied to habitants of the contiguous states of the United States. It will be used that way herein.
6. Diffie, Bailey W., and Justine Whitfield Bailey. *Porto Rico: A Broken Pledge*. Vanguard Press, New York, 1931.
7. Brown, Wenzell. *Dynamite on Our Doorstep*. Greenberg Publishers, New York, 1945, pp. 103 & 104. Reprinted with permission of Chilton Book Company, Radnor, Pennsylvania.
8. Jones, Clarence, and Rafael Pico. *Symposium on Geography of Puerto Rico*. University of Puerto Rico Press, Rio Piedras, P.R., 1955, Chapter II.
9. *World Almanac* 1971. Newspaper Enterprise Associates, Inc. pp. 409, 688.
10. Hanson, Earl Parker. *Puerto Rico: Ally for Progress*. D. Van Nostrand Co., p. 41.
11. *Ibid.*, p. 41.
12. *Ibid.*, pp. 36 ff.
13. *Ibid.*, p. 44.
14. Apparently this is also called the Milwaukee Deep.
15. In 1518 the Spanish Crown granted permission for Negroes (4,000) to be shipped to the islands of the Caribbean including Puerto Rico. Herring, Hubert. *Latin America*. Alfred Knopf, New York; 3rd edition, p. 105.
16. Lewis, Gordon K. *Puerto Rico: Freedom and Power in the Caribbean*. Monthly Review Press, New York, 1963, p. 28; Today the native rustic of the hill country (jíbaro) is the hero of Puerto Rican

culture, especially among the extreme *independentistas*. The extent to which his traits derive from the original Indians, Spanish conquerors, or Negro slaves is very much a moot question. By the 1540's the original Indians had been largely exterminated (apparently) by various kinds of labor abuse. This early period was characterized by constant racial friction, and . . . "Because of this conflict the aborigines were practically exterminated and this gave rise to the *jíbaro* who is in its large majority of pure Spanish blood. While the extermination of the Indians, giving occasion for the importation of slaves, accounts for the many *jíbaros* who spring from the mixture of Spaniards and Negroes . . . But, although the biological inheritance was small, culturally the Indian was as potent in forming the social inheritance of the jíbaro as the Spaniards themselves. The explanation for this phenomenon lies in the fact that the Spaniards who settled the island adjusted themselves to the environment. . . ." Rosario, José C. *The Development of the Puerto Rican Jíbaro and His Present Attitude Toward Society*. University of Puerto Rico Monograph, Series C, #1, pp. 17–18.

Chapter Two

1. This statement refers to the treatment of Negroes, Indians, and Chicanos in the U.S.

2. Chapman, Charles E. *Colonial Hispanic America: A History*. Macmillan & Co., New York, 1933, p. 34.

3. Hanke, Lewis. *All the People of the World Are Men*. James Ford Bell Lectures #8, University of Minnesota, Minneapolis, 1970; *Puerto Rico and the U.S.A.* Office of the Commonwealth of Puerto Rico. Washington, D.C., 1969, p. 4. (Hereafter cited as *Puerto Rico and the U.S.A.*)

4. *Latin America*. Alfred A. Knopf, New York, 1968, p. 25.

5. To emphasize man's tendency to exaggerate, Diffie points out that the population estimates of the island of Otaheite (Hawaii) ranged from 100,000 by Captain Cook, to 49,000 by the missionaries to 16,000 by Captain Wilson and only 5,000 by Turnbull. Diffie, B. W., and Justine W. Diffie. *Porto Rico: A Broken Pledge*. New York: Vanguard Press, 1931, p. 7; Diffie, B. W. *Latin American Civilization*. Harrisburg: Stockpole & Sons, 1945, p. 179; Wagenheim, Kal. *Puerto Rico*, Praeger, New York, 1970, p. 39.

6. *Boriquén* was the Indian name for island, therefore the Spaniards called the Indians *Boriqueños*. Steward, J. H., ed. *Handbook of South American Indians*. Washington, 1946–50. Vol. 4, p. 540.

7. On his return, Ponce was accompanied by Juan Garrido, a black freeman born in Angola. Later, Garrido sailed with Ponce when

he discovered Florida, and was possibly the first black migrant in North America.

8. The Taínos were docile and considered the Spaniards white gods. In 1510, however, some tested a Spaniard by submerging him in a stream for several hours. When the bloated corpse refused to revive, and "began to smell" the Indians finally decided the conquerors were mortal like themselves. Hanke, Lewis. *The First Social Experiments in America*. Peter Smith, Gloucester, Mass., 1964, pp. 68–69.

9. Haring, C. H. *The Spanish Empire in America*, Harcourt Brace & World Inc. (New York, 1947) is an excellent source for the administrative machinery of colonial Spain.

10. Diffie. *Colonial America*, p. 233.

11. It is questionable if Saint James ever was in Spain. Diffie, p. 234.

12. See map Frontispiece.

13. Lewis, *op. cit.*, p. 48.

14. Herring, *op. cit.*, pp. 199 ff. The restricting of the La Plata (Argentine) trade to the same route for years was even more stupid and vicious for that region.

15. Quoted in Hanke, Lewis. *The Spanish Struggle for Justice in the Conquest of America*. University of Pennsylvania Press, Philadelphia, 1949, pp. 17 ff.

16. Herring, *op. cit.*, p. 171; Diffie. *Latin America*, pp. 192–93.

17. Herring, *op. cit.*, p. 175.

18. Quoted in Hanke. *All the People of the World are Men*, p. 16; also see Morales Carrión, Arturo, "What is a Puerto Rican?" *The Island Times*, San Juan, Puerto Rico, Nov. 24, 1961, and Morales Carrión, Arturo, "Social Change and the Church in Latin America Today," *Bulletin, Commission of Ecumenical Mission and Relations of the United Presbyterian Church in the U.S.A.*, IV, #1, 1964.

19. *Puerto Rico and U.S.A.*, p. 12.

20. *Ibid.*, p. 12.

21. Lewis, *op. cit.*, p. 59. See also Hoetink, H. *Caribbean Race Relations: A Study of Two Variants*. Oxford University Press, New York, 1971.

22. Lewis, *op. cit.*, p. 116.

23. Maldonado Denis, Manuel. *Puerto Rico una interpretación histórico-social*. Editores Siglo XXI Mexico D.F., S.A., 1971, p. 7.

24. Maldonado Denis, p. 36.

25. Corretjer, Juan Antonio. *La Lucha por la Independencia de Puerto Rico*. Publicaciones de Union del Pueblo Pro Constitujente. San Juan de Puerto Rico, 1949, p. 1.

26. Wagenheim, *op. cit.*, p. 56.

27. Corretjer, *op. cit.*, p. 2.
28. Maldonado Denis, *op. cit.*, p. 38.
29. Lewis, *op. cit.*, p. 55.
30. Rosario, *op. cit.*, pp. 38–40.
31. Lewis, *op. cit.*, p. 53.
32. Lewis, *op. cit.*, p. 67.

Chapter Three

1. "Oh how beautiful it would be if Panama might become a modern 'Corinth.' That some day it might be our good fortune to establish a majestic assembly representing the republics, monarchies, and empires to discuss the important topics of peace and war with the other three parts of the world." Translated from Rodríguez, Cristóbal. *La República de Panamá y la Sociedad de las Naciones.* Panama City, Panama, 1929, p. 4.

2. The term Great American Desert was applied early to the semi-arid region lying to the west of the Mississippi.

3. The Monroe Doctrine as a term was really not used until the middle of the nineteenth century. Moreover, the rambling speech in which the concepts were first enunciated was actually the brainchild of John Quincy Adams—explained in more detail below. Bemis, Samuel F. *Latin American Policy of the United States.* Harcourt Brace & Co., New York, 1943, p. 63 ff.

4. Undoubtedly most of the early Americans, especially woodsmen and pioneers, considered it the design of "Providence" that the white man (especially Nordics) should expand and overrun the fertile lands and prairies. According to *Niles's Weekly Register* this concept was expressed as early as 1819: "They [the Floridas] belong to us as the county of Cornwall does to England: and besides, the sovereignty of them was found by experience to be indispensable to the safety of our citizens. . . ." It is difficult to determine exactly when the concept was first conceived. The term itself, however, was apparently first used in the *Democratic Review* and *New York Morning News* in 1845 by John L. O'Sullivan who claimed it was "our destiny to overspread and possess the whole of the continent which Providence has given us." Bailey, Thomas. *Diplomatic History of the American People.* F. S. Crofts, New York, 1947, p. 176; Pratt, J. W. "Origin of Manifest Destiny," *American Historical Review*, Vol. 32.

5. *Scientific American* (1882), Vol. 14, No. 347, p. 5530.

6. The last rail was laid January 27, 1855, a Sunday; and the chief engineer, Colonel Totten, decided to send the first locomotive over the line. But "retaining some of his Puritan notions of respect for the Sabbath" he did it with the slogan "the better the day the

better the deed." Up to 1885 the total cost had been approximately $7,000,000, whereas earnings taken in were $2,125,232.31. Hauberg, Clifford A. *Economic & Social Development in Panama, 1849–1880.* Unpublished thesis. University of Minnesota, April 1950, p. 196.

7. Commager, H. S. *The Study of History.* Charles & Merritt Books, Columbus, Ohio, p. 4.

8. The so-called [President James K.] Polk Corollary was promulgated to prevent voluntary transfer of territory by an American state to any European power. Dozer, Donald M., *The Monroe Doctrine.* Alfred A. Knopf, New York, 1965, Introduction, p. 10.

9. Mack, Gerstle. *The Land Divided: A History of the Panama Canal.* Alfred A. Knopf, New York, 1944, p. 419.

10. By the Clayton-Bulwer Treaty (contrary to the Monroe Doctrine concept) the U.S. had recognized the equal and joint interest of Great Britain in the Isthmian area should a canal be built.

11. By this proposal the United States offered Colombia $10,000,000 cash and $250,000 annually for a strip six miles wide, including the Panama Railroad property. E. Taylor Parks in a scholarly study, *Colombia and the U.S., 1765–1934,* Durham, N.C., 1935, concludes that Colombia stood to lose $50,000,000 if the treaty were negotiated with the U.S., rather than wait and acquire the French concession by default.

12. Before the United States would evacuate Cuba after the Spanish American War, it forced upon Cuba the Platt Amendment which made that country a protectorate of the United States. Bailey, *op. cit.*, p. 548 ff.

13. Perkins, Dexter. *Hands Off. A History of the Monroe Doctrine.* Little Brown & Co., Preface.

14. An exception to this would be the Clayton-Bulwer Treaty of 1850 which recognized the joint rights of Great Britain to any Canal that might be built in Central America. At that particular time the United States was especially preoccupied with the slavery issue at home. The Clayton-Bulwer Treaty was finally abrogated by the Hay-Pauncefote Treaty of 1902.

15. Bemis, Samuel Flagg. *Latin American Policy of the United States.* Harcourt Brace & Co., New York, 1943, p. 120.

16. Bemis, *ibid.*, p. 153.

17. Salvador de Madariaga quoted in the preface of Dozer, Donald M., *op. cit.* Such criticism ranges from early writings of José Enrique Rodó, Uruguayan essayist (1872–1917), who dwelt on the materialism of American democracy in his masterpiece *Ariel*, to the publications of Miguel Angel Asturias, Guatemalan (awarded the Nobel Prize for Literature for 1967), whose works "scathingly criticize Latin American

dictatorship and 'Yankee Imperialism.' " *New York Times*, October 20, 1967, pp. 1, 44.

18. Bemis, *op. cit.*, pp. 135 ff; Bailey, *op. cit.*, pp. 506 ff.

Chapter Four

1. Some "100% Americans" might object to the term "Broken Promises." It should be noted that one of the most scholarly treatments of this period 1898–1930, is by the Diffies and is termed *Porto Rico: A Broken Pledge*.

2. Aitkin, Thomas Jr. *Poet in the Fortress*. New American Library, New York, New York. 1964, pp. 25, 26; Wagenheim, *op. cit.*, p. 63; Diffie, B. W., *op. cit.*, pp. 20, 21.

3. Numerous cases involving the status of islands which came under U.S. jurisdiction were brought to the Supreme Court of the United States.

4. Lewis, *op. cit.*, p. 110.

5. Chapman, C. E. *A History of the Cuban Republic: A Study in Hispanic American Politics*. Macmillan, New York, 1927, p. 194; Hauberg, C. A. *Latin American Revolutions*. T. S. Denison, Minneapolis, 1968, p. 190.

6. Diffie, *op. cit.*, p. 20.

7. In 1903 the University of Puerto Rico was established.

8. Lewis, *op. cit.*, p. 103.

9. Senator Foraker insisted that he had included this provision to protect the island from inroads of outside influence; there is reason to think, however, that he did it at the request of the beet sugar lobby which feared the rise of a significant cane sugar industry.

10. Diffie, *op. cit.*, p. 74.

11. Hanson, *op. cit.*, p. 89.

12. Diffie, *op. cit.*, p. 166.

13. Lewis, *op. cit.*, p. 92.

14. Diffie, *op. cit.*, p. 90.

15. Diffie, *op. cit.*, p. 104.

16. Lewis, *op. cit.*, p. 88.

17. Mathews, Thomas. *Puerto Rican Politics and the New Deal*. University of Florida Press, Gainesville, Fla., 1960, p. 7.

18. Diffie, *op. cit.*, pp. 5 ff.

19. Mathews, *op. cit.*, p. 11.

Chapter Five

1. Mathews, *op. cit.*, p. 19. Much of the material in this chapter comes from that source.

2. In the earlier period the status issue involved the two alternatives—colonial status or independence. After the Commonwealth was created (1952) the situation became more complex.

3. The extreme Nationalist Party had polled only 329 votes in the previous 1928 election, and it appeared impossible for it to secure 10 percent of the previous vote total or 30,000 signatures to be eligible for the ballot. After an attempt by the legislature to legalize the party by law was unsuccessful, the Nationalists "managed" to secure 30,000 signatures. In the actual vote of the 1932 election that party secured less than 10,000 votes which must have been as embarrassing to the Union-Republican group as to the Nationalists. Apparently the Coalition group had favored the ballot privilege for the Nationalists to split the independence vote between Liberals and Nationalists. Mathews, *op. cit.*, pp. 35, 44.

4. Mathews, *op. cit.*, p. 15.

5. Mathews, *op. cit.*, p. 53.

6. Mathews, *op. cit.*, p. 47.

7. Miss Black was an accomplished journalist in Washington, D.C., who was very sympathetic toward Puerto Rico and served as unofficial lobbyist for Muñoz Marín. By knowledgeable writers including Robert S. Allen of the "Washington-Merry-go Round" fame, she was rated one of the best.

8. Mathews, *op. cit.*, p. 5.

9. Mathews, *op. cit.*, p. 56.

10. Up to this time Puerto Rico was the responsibility of the Secretary of War (George Dern in 1933). In the spring of 1934 the President transferred authority to the Secretary of the Interior so that the situation would be similar to that of Alaska, Hawaii, and the Virgin Islands.

11. Mathews, *op. cit.*, p. 66.

12. Mathews, *op. cit.*, p. 71.

13. Mathews, *op. cit.*, p. 78.

14. Mathews, *op. cit.*, p. 101.

15. Mathews, *op. cit.*, p. 81.

16. Mathews, *op. cit.*, p. 108.

17. Quoted in Mathews *op. cit.*, p. 98.

18. Mathews, *op. cit.*, p. 323.

19. Mathews, *op. cit.*, p. 72.

20. It should be pointed out that neither Tugwell nor Muñoz Marín was opposed to sugar enterprises utilizing over 500 acres per se; they were opposed when the profits went to absentee-owned corporations.

21. Mathews, *op. cit.*, p. 187.

22. Nationalist Party members, incensed at the prison terms to

which Albizu Campos (prominent and extreme Nationalist leader) and seven others were subjected, planned a series of demonstrations on a peace day, Palm Sunday, March 21, 1937. Other such parades and meetings had been stopped by the police under orders from the governor. In this case permission to march in peaceful protest had been granted by the Mayor of Ponce and security steps were at first taken by the governor's agents. At the last "minute," the morning of Palm Sunday, the mayor's permit was canceled by Governor Winship in a rather arbitrary manner. The Nationalists insisted that the cancellation had arrived too late and the parade began peacefully. The town worshipers stopped to watch on their way home from church and the holiday atmosphere was characterized by palm leaves, girls in starched white dresses and neat boys in white shirts, black trousers, and small caps.

A captain of the police stepped into the street and ordered a halt— there was tenseness, then a shot rang out and this was followed by screams, curses, and panic: "This was the Ponce Massacre, a disgrace whose repercussions reached into the White House and finally wrote the termination of Governor Winship's regime." (Aitkin, Jr., *op cit.*, p. 113).

The horrible event was followed by investigations, survey commissions, and a trial. No one was ever able to place the blame for the initial shooting and the Nationalist defendants were acquitted. The cause of justice and the defense of the weak had been served. The trial also brought fame to the lawyer, Ramos Antonini, for his genius in defense of the accused. This in turn, led to lasting friendship between Muñoz Marín and Antonini and the latter's great talents consequently were placed at the disposal of the party of Muñoz. Today, March 21 in Puerto Rico is remembered as the anniversary of La Masacre de Ponce.

23. Goodsell, Charles T. *Administrators of a Revolution: Executive Reform in Puerto Rico under Governor Tugwell, 1941–1946.* Harvard University Press, Cambridge, 1965, p. 3.

24. Goodsell, Charles T., *op. cit.*, p. 5.

Chapter Six

1. Doubleday & Co., New York, 1958, pp. 17, 43.
2. Hanson, *op. cit.*, p. 16.
3. *El Mundo*, Jan. 24, 1934; quoted in Mathews, *op. cit.*, p. 152.
4. Mathews, *op. cit.*, p. 299.
5. *El Batey* refers to the sugar-making machinery of the *centrales* but in this context it took on the Indian meaning and referred to a Sunday family gathering and a native forum.

6. Much of the material on this campaign is taken from *Poet in the Fortress* by Thomas Aitkin, Jr. New American Library, New York, 1964, Chapter X.

7. Aitkin, *op. cit.*, p. 137. Henry Wells has probably contributed the best explanation of why Muñoz changed from being concerned primarily with independence to minimizing the political status issue and stressing reform and progress in the general welfare area. In the campaign of 1940 Muñoz discovered that the *jíbaros* had a deep yearning for a better life for themselves and children and were not disturbed by the prospect of a close relationship with the U.S. Apparently he learned that a great many of the peasant "hillbillies" preferred a "close association with their fellow citizens of the American Union and with all men on earth. . . ." They also had a true sense of individual worth and dignity. As one poor *jíbaro* put it when he refused to sell his vote to a deputy he didn't like—"I am the master of my hunger. . . ." Wells, Henry. *The Modernization of Puerto Rico.* Harvard University Press, Cambridge, Mass., 1969. Chapter 6, "Breakthrough Toward Modernity," and pp. 26, 125.

8. Aitkin, *op. cit.*, p. 140.

9. Lewis, *op. cit.*, p. 148.

10. Aitkin, *op. cit.*, p. 134.

11. *Ibid.*, p. 135.

12. Aitkin, *op. cit.*, p. 143.

13. In the House, the *Populares* and the Coalition group both had eighteen seats. The newly formed Tripartite Party held the balance. Apparently Muñoz was able to maneuver these as well as a few Coalition members for support of his program.

14. Aitkin, *op. cit.*, p. 149.

Muñoz Marín's political triumph of 1940 was accompanied by a major change in his personal life. During and as a result of his political activities he met Inéz Mendoza who replaced Muna Lee as his marital companion. Their home on Isla Verde had already witnessed the birth of a daughter, Viviana. Another was named Victoria in honor of the successful campaign.

Muna Lee, Muñoz's earlier wife, returned to the States where she continued a career dedicated to promoting goodwill in the Americas. Muñoz secured a divorce from his first wife and married Inéz Mendoza in 1947. From afar Muna Lee continued to be a loyal devotee of Muñoz. Aitkin, *op. cit.*, p. 145.

15. Goodsell, *op. cit.*, p. 15.

16. It has become part of American folklore to associate significant revolutionary change with the Communists. Therefore it should be stressed that Muñoz Marín got little or no support from this group.

In fact, the Communists, being very weak in Puerto Rico, were not legally recognized until 1935. They were of course extremely critical of the Coalition whom they considered capitalist. The Socialists, who had started "red," were also criticized because they had betrayed the proletariat in a "yellow" manner. With the Nationalists, the Communists agreed on independence, but, they too were criticized for ignoring the class struggle. Mathews, *op. cit.*, pp. 305–306.

17. Tugwell's acceptance of the University post as Chancellor at the request of Muñoz Marín now seems ill-considered. There was heated opposition registered on the part of students and *politicos*. As a result Tugwell resigned before becoming governor.

18. Tugwell, Rexford G. *The Stricken Land: The Story of Puerto Rico*. Doubleday & Co., New York, 1947, p. 142. (Hereafter cited as S. L.) The viciousness of party politics is illustrated by the comment of Taft considered in juxtaposition to Tugwell's practical contributions in the area of effective administration in Puerto Rico. At Gainesville, Florida, this writer observed one Caribbean Conference dedicated to the enlightened leadership of Rexford G. Tugwell. A leading United States philosopher once characterized Senator Taft as a person who came through college with all A's but little knowledge!

19. *Ah bendito* had many meanings, ranging from mild concern to great but hopeless indignation. If, for example, the inefficient water system was due to neglect by officials who were lazy, corrupt, and incompetent and one complained, the answer might be, "*Ah bendito*, but they have large families and must work."

20. Aitkin, Jr., *op. cit.*, pp. 163, 194.

21. Goodsell, *op. cit.*, p. 149.

22. Tugwell, *op. cit.*, p. 646.

23. Lewis, *op. cit.*, p. 158.

24. At an earlier time of political struggle, Don Luis Muñoz Rivera, a poet and father of Muñoz Marín, had written a poem called *Sisyphus*. This is a reference to a Grecian myth which describes the task of Sisyphus. In Hades Sisyphus was forever condemned to roll a huge stone uphill which once arriving at the top would roll downhill. Aitkin, Jr., *op. cit.*, pp. 28 ff.

Chapter Seven

1. Aitkin, *op. cit.*, pp. 174–77.

2. Goodsell, *op. cit.*, p. 183.

3. The Spanish verb *fomentar* signifies promotion and *fomento* is often used to denote the department concerned with internal development. In Puerto Rico after 1942 it was called the Development Company and later changed to Puerto Rican Industrial Development

Company. *Fomento* often refers to the whole program Operation Bootstrap. Goodsell, *op. cit.*, pp. 174–76.

4. Goodsell, *op. cit.*, p. 186.

5. "Service activities" here refers primarily to what Goodsell calls "social overhead capital"—pure water, communications, electric power, transportation, and the social infrastructure in general. Goodsell, *op. cit.*, p. 174. But it can also include those activities which result in the betterment of living standards—housing, health, education, and general cultural improvement.

6. *Puerto Rico, U.S.A.*, p. 25.

7. *Puerto Rico, U.S.A.*, p. 31.

8. Tugwell, *Art of Politics*, p. 68.

9. Goodsell, *op. cit.*, p. 55.

10. Tugwell, quoted in Goodsell, *op. cit.*, p. 55.

11. Probably no one did more to further Puerto Rican enlightened government than Tugwell. Having come to the conclusion that Congressional cooperation would not be enhanced by his presence at *La Fortaleza* and that possibly even the governor being elected might be delayed, Tugwell made the grand gesture and resigned. Previously he had quietly informed both Muñoz and the President of his plans. Some of his critics, however, appreciated neither his great contributions nor his altruism and attributed his resignation to Puerto Rican opposition. Aitkin, Jr., *op. cit.*, p. 176.

12. Aitkin, *op. cit.*, p. 202.

13. Semasiology indicates that words can take various meanings and this is one of the most significant concepts from *Through the Looking Glass* which seems very pertinent here:

"When *I* use a word," Humpty Dumpty said, in rather a scornful tone, "it means just what I choose it to mean—neither more nor less."

"The question is," said Alice, "whether you *can* make words mean so many different things."

"The question is," said Humpty Dumpty, "which is to be master—that's all." . . . "When I make a word do a lot of work like that," said Humpty Dumpty, "I always pay it extra." Carroll, Lewis. (Pseud.) *Through the Looking Glass*. Heritage Press, 1941, pp. 112–13.

14. Quoted in *Puerto Rico, U.S.A.*, p. 20.

Chapter Eight

1. "Puerto Rico: Our Backyard Colony," Michael Meyerson. *Ramparts*, June 1970, p. 51. (Copyright Noah's Ark, Inc.)

2. Hereafter continentals refers to people from the 50 states of the United States.

3. Lewis, *op. cit.*, p. 9.

4. Mintz, Sidney W. "Puerto Rican Emigration: A threefold Comparison," *Social and Economic Studies.* 4 (Dec., 1955), pp. 311–25.

5. Senior, Clarence. *The Puerto Ricans, Strangers—Then Neighbors*, Quadrangle Books, Chicago, 1961, p. 86.

6. Chenault, Lawrence R. *The Puerto Rican Migrant in New York City.* Russell & Russell, New York, 1970, p. 53.

7. Glazer, Nathan, and Daniel Moynihan. *Beyond the Melting Pot: The Negroes, Puerto Ricans, Jews, Italians, and Irish of New York City.* MIT Press, Cambridge, 1962, p. 91. Chenault, *op. cit.*, pp. 91, 92.

8. Glazer and Moynihan, *op. cit.*, p. 93. It is interesting to note a sharp decline in those Puerto Ricans categorized as Negro—perhaps a trend of census takers in listing mixed Puerto Ricans as white. Thus a sharp reduction is observed in those who are considered, or consider themselves, black from 1940 when 11 percent of the Puerto Ricans in New York City were listed as black, to 1960 when the proportion of blacks among the Puerto Ricans was listed as 4 percent.

9. Glazer and Moynihan, *op. cit.*, p. 93.

10. "Higher visibility" of the stranger may arise from speech, clothing, color, behavior, and other factors.

11. Senior, *op. cit.*, p. 37.

12. Hernández, Joseph W., "The Sociological Implications of Return Migration in Puerto Rico: An Exploratory Study." Unpublished Doctoral Thesis. University of Minnesota, July, 1964, p. 62; Senior, *op. cit.*, pp. 37–40, and Chenault, *op. cit.*, pp. 53, 54.

13. Those who travel to and from Puerto Rico are known as a "floating population," i.e., tourists, visitors, military men, and businessmen, etc. A recent work by José Hernández Alvarez, *Return Migration in Puerto Rico.* (Social Science Research Center, University of Puerto Rico, 1964, p. 7) estimates the figure of returning Puerto Ricans at 83,000 between 1955 and 1963.

14. Wagenheim, *op. cit.*, p. 169.

15. Wagenheim, *op. cit.*, p. 158.

16. Wagenheim, *op. cit.*, p. 130.

17. Senior, *op. cit.*, p. 89.

18. Lewis, *op. cit.*, p. 9.

19. Senior, *op. cit.*, p. 92.

20. Chenault, *op. cit.*, p. 52.

21. *Puerto Rico, U.S.A.*, p. 44.

22. Senior & Watkins, *op. cit.*, p. 699.

23. House of Representatives, May 4 & June 4, 1971.

Chapter Nine

1. Senior and Watkins, *op. cit.*, p. 705.

2. *Puerto Rico, U.S.A.*, p. 44.

3. Senior and Watkins, *op. cit.*, pp. 706–7.

4. The particular labor shortages of the Industrial East, especially New York City, are the result of a combination of factors. In 1924, the Immigration Act of that year cut off the influx of workers from Europe. The supply of cheap labor from the South was not sufficient. Also, the older immigrant groups were undergoing social mobility and were restive under their present status.

5. Senior and Watkins, *op. cit.*, p. 706.

6. Census definitions include only first- and second-generation migrants. Increasing numbers of third-generation Puerto Ricans are no longer counted.

7. "The Puerto Ricans," *Newsweek*, June 15, 1970. Vol. 75, p. 92. *Plátanos* and *yautías* are food products favored by Puerto Ricans.

8. Senior and Watkins, *op. cit.*, p. 703.

9. Mills, C. Wright, Senior, Clarence, and Goldsen, Rose Kohn. *The Puerto Rican Journey: New York's Newest Migrants.* Harper & Bros., New York, 1950, p. 56.

10. Wagenheim, *op. cit.*, p. 193.

11. Hernandez-Alvarez, José. "The Movement and Settlement of Puerto Rican Migrants within the United States, 1950–1960," *International Migration Review*, 2 (Spring, 1968), 50.

12. Senior and Watkins, *op. cit.*, p. 696.

13. Hernandez-Alvarez, José, *op. cit.*, p. 44.

14. In New York City the mean rate of Puerto Rican density per tract (a particular demographic measurement of area) was 31.3 percent, whereas 18.5 percent was the corresponding figure for tracts in other cities.

15. Hernandez-Alvarez, José, *op. cit.*, p. 51.

16. Hernandez-Alvarez, José, *op. cit.*, p. 51.

17. Macisco, John J., "The Assimilation of the Puerto Ricans on the Mainland: a Socio-Demographic Approach," *International Migration Review*, 2 (Spring, 1968), pp. 24, 31.

18. Macisco, *op. cit.*, p. 32.

19. Badillo, Herman, *Congressional Record.* June 7, 1971.

20. Howard, John R., *Awakening Minorities, American Indians, Mexican Americans, Puerto Ricans.* Aldine Publishing Company, Chicago, 1970, p. 126.

21. Glazer and Moynihan, *op. cit.*, pp. 94, 95. Morris Eagle's article, "The Puerto Ricans in New York," in Nathan Glazer and Davis McEntire (eds.), *Studies in Housing and Minority Groups*,

University of California Press, Berkeley, 1960, presents a detailed study of the spread of Puerto Ricans throughout New York City.

22. Senior, *op. cit.*, p. 48.

23. Howard, *op. cit.*, pp. 128, 129.

24. Howard, *op. cit.*, p. 126.

25. Howard, *op. cit.*, p. 127.

26. "The Puerto Ricans," *Newsweek*, June 15, 1970, p. 93.

27. *Ibid.*, p. 93.

28. Wagenheim, *op. cit.*, p. 194.

29. *Newsweek*, June 15, 1970, p. 93.

30. See above Part I, Chapter II.

31. Note study of Joseph P. Fitzpatrick, "Attitudes of Puerto Ricans toward Color," *American Catholic Sociological Review*, Vol. 20, No. 3 (Fall), 1959, pp. 219–33.

32. Howard, *op. cit.*, p. 130. As we have already indicated, slavery was probably not any more humane in Puerto Rico than elsewhere in the nineteenth century. Possibly the same is true of racial prejudice for the earlier period as well as today. In a recent article Samuel Betances points out that even Celso Barbosa was inconsistent in his reaction to this problem—claiming at one and the same time that there was no prejudice of race or color but being concerned enough to write how to "solve" it. Betances concludes by pointing out that upper-class status in Puerto Rico seems to be determined by a ". . . 'physical ideal' of white skin, apart from educational or economic achievement, and that since this aspect can be labeled racist, Puerto Ricans find it difficult to claim that what exists in Puerto Rico is simply a process of social and class discrimination." Betances, Samuel, "The Prejudice of Having Prejudice in Puerto Rico." *The Rican*, Winter 1972, pp. 41–44.

33. Mills, C. Wright, Senior, Clarence, and Goldsen, Rose Kohn, *op. cit.*, pp. 133–34.

34. Thomas, Piri. *Down These Mean Streets*, Alfred A. Knopf, New York, 1967.

35. *Newsweek*, June 15, 1970, p. 93.

36. Trejo, Arnulfo D. "The Puerto Ricans," *Wilson Library Bulletin*, March 1970, p. 721.

Chapter Ten

1. Conflicting findings regarding Puerto Rican migration make it quite impossible to be absolutely accurate. This undoubtedly results (as already indicated) from confused criteria in census-taking standards. Obviously this applies to black and white categories but could affect other classifications also. The accuracy of the 1970

census is even disputed. September 8, 1971, *The New York Times* carried an article, "Migration Study Urged by Badillo," claiming census figures were insufficient. Peter Kihss reported much the same thing April 20, 1972, in *The New York Times.*

2. Sedentes is found neither in regular Spanish nor in the English dictionary. It comes from the Latin verb sedens and means *Que esta sentado* (that which is setting) or sedentary. *Diccionario de la lengua española.* 19th ed. (1970).

3. *The Commonwealth Bureau of Labor Statistics.* 1958–1962.

4. Statistics indicate the significant change taking place. The number of Puerto Ricans classified as non-white has declined each decade from 1940 until 1960. In 1940 it was 13 percent; in 1950 it was 8 percent and in 1960, 4 percent. The shift is most likely the result of change in the method of data collection. In the 1960 census the respondent classified himself according to categories of white and non-white.

5. All authorities do not agree on educational statistics. It must also be remembered that the migrant is part of a select group.

6. Macisco, John J., *op. cit.*, p. 27. See also Senior, *The Puerto Ricans,* pp. 94–96.

7. Postman, Neil (& Weingartner, Charles). *Teaching as a Subversive Activity.* Delacorte Press, 1969, Chapter I, pp. 1–15.

8. Fitzpatrick, Joseph P., "Puerto Ricans in Perspective: The Meaning of Migration to the Mainland," *The International Migration Review.* 2 (Spring 1968) 7–19.

9. Wagenheim, *op. cit.*, p. 193.

10. No farm-labor recruitment is allowed in Puerto Rico unless it is done via the Puerto Rican Employment Service and according to these regulations:

1) No fees may be charged the worker or employer.
2) Employment service will accept only those orders for workers which have been put through the clearance procedures.
3) The firm signs an agreement with the worker only under provisions which have been approved by the secretary of labor.
4) Two major requirements of the work agreement are that there must be a life and accident policy to cover the worker during the plane trip and a guarantee of 160 hours of pay for each four weeks of work.
5) Wages offered must be those being paid in the area for the same or comparable work performed.
6) Workmen's Compensation coverage must be provided,

either through a state fund, where one exists, or through private policies.

7) Medical services for off-the-job accidents and illness must be provided, whether through direct facilities or through the use of a group insurance plan to which the workers contribute.

8) The employer must furnish adequate housing, rent-free.

9) There shall be no discrimination against the workers because of race, color, religion, or union activity.

Castaño, Carlos, "The Puerto Rican Migratory Program." *Makers of America—Emergent Minorities. Encyclopaedia Britannica.* William Benton, Publisher, 1970, Vol. X, pp. 27–29.

11. Aitkin, Jr., *op. cit.*, p. 196.

12. *Puerto Rico U.S.A.*, p. 45.

13. It is important to bear in mind the numerous home-based industries on the island and the large proportion of women engaged in the garment industry in New York City.

14. Senior, *op. cit.*, p. 90.

15. Senior, *op. cit.*, p. 106.

16. Lopez, Lillian, "New York: The South Bronx Project," *Wilson Library Bulletin.* March 1970, p. 757.

17. Lopez, Lillian, *op. cit.*, p. 759.

18. "Job Plan Helpful to Puerto Ricans," *New York Times,* June 1, 1971.

19. Lopez, *op. cit.*, p. 722.

20. Wagenheim, *op. cit.*, p. 164.

21. This movement is often fundamentalist in nature, emphasizing the Holy Spirit, uninhibited religious feeling, and sometimes motivates "speaking in tongues."

22. Wakefield, Dan, *Island in the City: Puerto Ricans in New York.* Corinth Publishing Co., New York, 1957, pp. 52, 53.

23. Wakefield, *op. cit.*, pp. 62, 63.

24. Those who have little are the ones that are here.

25. Glazer and Moynihan, *op. cit.*, p. 118.

26. Herman Badillo, the first Puerto Rican to be elected to Congress, may be a sign that political parties are becoming aware of the Puerto Rican latent political potential and that Puerto Ricans are becoming somewhat conscious of their own powers.

27. Wakefield, *op. cit.*, pp. 128, 129.

28. Browning, Frank, "From Rumble to Revolution: The Young Lords," *Ramparts,* Oct. 1970, p. 19.

29. Browning, Frank, *op. cit.*, p. 25.

30. Browning, Frank, *op. cit.*, p. 25.

31. Browning, Frank, *op. cit.*, p. 23.

32. *Newsweek*, June 15, 1970, p. 94.

33. Padilla, Elena. *Up From Puerto Rico*. Columbia Press, New York, 1958, p. 57.

34. *Newsweek*, June 15, 1970, p. 94.

Chapter Eleven

1. Senior, C., *op. cit.*, p. 53.

2. Senior, C., *op. cit.*, p. 76. In this chapter the lives and achievements of some individuals will be treated at length in three areas—sports, the acting profession, and a third which will include education, statesmen, and public administrators. Obviously all individuals cannot be treated here. Therefore, those chosen might be considered especially significant in terms of example and leadership.

3. Chi Chi was a nickname taken after Rodríguez's childhood idol—baseball hero Chi Chi Flores.

4. *Current Biography Yearbook*. Moritz, Charles (ed.), H. W. Wilson Co., New York, 1969, p. 370.

5. He donated a quarter of the $20,000 prize to a relief fund for tornado victims in the Midwest.

6. Dan Jenkins in *Sports Illustrated* (Aug. 10, 1964), p. 34. Rodríguez, when time permits, does give young Puerto Ricans free golf instruction. *Current Biography Yearbook*, pp. 371, 372.

7. *Minneapolis Tribune*, July 20, 1971, p. 1 C.

8. "Clemente a Star with Capacity for Involvement," *New York Times*, January 2, 1973, p. 48 C; *Latin American Times*, January 10, 1973, pp. 1, 5.

9. *Time*, January 15, 1973, pp. 42–43.

10. "Roberto Clemente: Death of a Proud Man," *Sports Illustrated*, January 15, 1973.

11. *New York Times*, January 3, 1973, p. 17 C.

12. *New York Times*, March 21, 1973, pp. 31, 34.

13. *Current Biography Yearbook*, 1968, p. 85; *Sports Illustrated*, July 24, 1967.

14. Inasmuch as Cardinals is plural, the Spanish equivalent should be *Los* (plural) *Birdos* rather than *El* (singular). Spanglish, however, is a mixture of the two languages and apparently doesn't require grammatical perfection.

15. *Minneapolis Tribune*, Wednesday, July 21, 1971, p. 3 C.

16. The stunning victory of the *Populares* in the 1972 fall elections sent Benítez to Washington, D.C. as Resident Commissioner.

17. *Current Biography Yearbook*, Moritz, Charles (ed.). H. W. Wilson Co., New York, 1963, p. 285. *Newsweek*, February 19, 1962.

18. Speech in the U.S. House of Representatives, May 4, 1971. Obtained during private correspondence with H. Badillo.

19. Rand, Christopher. *The Puerto Ricans*, Oxford University Press, New York, 1958, p. 62.

20. Rand, *op. cit.*, p. 62.

21. Wagenheim, *op. cit.*, p. 148. A *papelito* is a "little slip of paper."

Retrospect and Prospects

1. Aitken, Jr., *op. cit.*, p. 225.

2. Thomas, Piri, *op. cit.*, p. 180.

3. *Ibid.*, p. 296.

4. Aside from the Preamble, Article I, Section 8, states specifically: Congress shall have power: To lay and collect taxes etc. . . . and provide for the common defense and general welfare of the United States.

5. Browning, Frank, "From Rumble to Revolution: The Young Lords," *Ramparts*, Oct. 1970; "Identity Crisis," *Newsweek*, Jan. 19, 1970; "House of Studies," (taken from *U.S. Journal*: San Juan, Puerto Rico) in the *New Yorker*, Feb. 14, 1960.

6. Muñoz Marín, Luis, "Breakthrough from Nationalism," *Godkin Lectures* (Harvard), April 1959.

7. Quoted in Mayer, Milton, *On Liberty: Man vs. the State*, Center for the Study of Democratic Institutions, Santa Barbara, Calif., 1969, p. 142.

8. Quoted in a speech by Resident Commissioner Jorge L. Cordova at Hotel San Juan, March 26, 1971. *Citizenship*. Puerto Rican Booklet Series #7, Office of the Commonwealth, Washington, D.C., May 1971.

9. Aitkin, Jr., *op. cit.*, p. 196.

10. According to the present (1971) Resident Commissioner, it is a moot question just how the Peoples' 10 percent will vote in 1972. "I might . . . [point] out that there is a real question whether the 10% vote obtained by the Peoples' Party would have been cast for the Popular Democratic Party or for the New Progressive Party in 1968 if the Peoples' Party had not been formed." Letter from Jorge L. Cordova, Puerto Rican Resident Commissioner, November 18, 1971.

The administration of Roberto Sanchez Villela (1965–1969) was marred by his involvement in personal scandal—an affaire de coeur—as well as growing friction between Muñoz Marín and the incumbent. This caused many to look with jaundiced eye on the future of the Commonwealth as well as the continued success of the Popular Party. During the last years of the Luis Ferré administration (1969–1973) popular forecasts indicated that the New Progressive Party (statehood) would win over the pro-commonwealth *Populares* by an approximate 44 percent to 40 percent margin. It came as a surprise, therefore, when the Popular Democratic candidate, 36-year-old Rafael Hernandez-Colón, won the governorship by a rather overwhelming and unexpected majority. In addition to the governorship, the *Populares* captured both houses of the legislature, the office of resident commissioner in Washington, D.C., as well as 72 of the 78 municipalities. It would appear that the election results might be viewed as a "reaffirmation of the people of Puerto Rico in the commonwealth status rather than statehood or independence"—despite alleged corruption and recounts carried out in Puerto Rico after the election. *New York Times*, November 9, 1972, p. 15; *San Juan Star*, November 15, 1972, p. 3; November 16, p. 1; Wells, Henry, *op. cit.*, Chapter 14.

11. Mayer, *op. cit.*, p. 129.

12. Cordova, Resident Commissioner, *op. cit.*

13. *Minneapolis Tribune*, August 11, 1971. One should probably emphasize that which is obvious, that the progress Ferré stresses is more the result of past planning (Operation Bootstrap) than that of the current administration.

14. Meyerson, Michael, "Puerto Rico: Our Backward Colony," *Ramparts*, June 1970; Lewis, Oscar, "One Can Suffer Anywhere," *Harpers*, May 1969; "Identity Crisis," *Newsweek*, January 12, 1970.

15. *Congressional Record*, Friday, June 4, 1971.

16. Goodsell, Charles T., "Puerto Rico Moves Forward," *Current History*, December 1966, pp. 321–26.

Selected Bibliography

GUIDES AND AIDS

HILTON, RONALD. *Hispanic-American Reports*. Stanford University, 1946–1964, Stanford, California.
————. *Who's Who in Latin America* (3rd Ed.), Stanford, California, 1940–1951.
Handbook of Latin American Studies, published annually, Gainesville, Florida.
HERRING, HUBERT. *A History of Latin America*. New York: Alfred A. Knopf, 3rd edition, 1968.
Puerto Rico–U.S.A. Office of the Commonwealth of Puerto Rico, 2210 R Street, Northwest, Washington, D.C.
Latin American Studies. Latin American Institute, Rutgers University. State University of N. Y.
Times of the Americas. Washington, D.C.
TORRES-RECOSECO, ARTURO. *The Epic of Latin American Literature*. Oxford University Press, New York, 1942.
MORITZ, CHARLES (ed.). *Current Biography Yearbook*. New York: H. W. Wilson Co.

BOOKS

AITKIN, THOMAS, JR. *Poet in the Fortress: The Story of Luis Muñoz Marín*. New York: New American Library, 1964.
ALEXANDER, ROBERT J. *Communism in Latin America*. New Brunswick: Rutgers University Press, 1957.
————. *Prophets of Revolution* (Profile of Latin American Leaders). New York: Macmillan Co., 1962.
ANDERSON, ROBERT W. *Party Politics in Puerto Rico*. Stanford: Stanford University Press, 1965.
BEMIS, SAMUEL F. *Latin American Policy of the United States*. Harcourt, Brace & Co., New York, 1943.
BERBUSSE, EDWARD J. *The United States and Puerto Rico, 1898–1900*. Chapel Hill: University of North Carolina Press, 1966.
BERLE, BEATRICE BISHOP. *80 Puerto Rican Families in New York City: Health and Disease Studies in Context*. New York: Columbia University Press, 1958.

[195]

BRAMELD, THEODORE. *The Remaking of a Culture: Life and Education in Puerto Rico.* New York: John Wiley & Sons, Inc., 1959.

BROWN, WENZELL. *Dynamite on our Doorstep.* New York: Greenberg Publishers, 1945.

BURMA, JOHN H. *Spanish-Speaking Groups in the United States.* Durham: Duke University Press, 1954.

BURNETT, ELAINE H. (Ed.). *One Spark from Holocaust* (The Crisis in Latin America). Center for the Study of Democratic Institutions Fund for the Republic, Inc., 1972.

CHAPMAN, CHARLES E. *Colonial Hispanic America: A History.* New York: Macmillan, 1933.

————. *A History of the Cuban Republic: A Study in Hispanic American Policies.* New York: Macmillan, 1927.

CHENAULT, LAWRENCE R. *The Puerto Rican Migrant in New York City.* New York: Russell & Russell, 1938.

CORRETJER, JUAN ANTONIO. *La Lucha Por la Independencia de Puerto Rico.* San Juan: Publicaciones de Union del Pueblo Pro Constituyente, 1949.

CROWTHER, SAMUEL. *The Romance and Rise of the American Tropics.* New York: Doubleday, Doran & Co., Inc., 1927.

DIFFIE, BAILEY W. and DIFFIE, JUSTINE WHITEFIELD. *Porto Rico: A Broken Pledge.* New York: The Vanguard Press, 1931.

DIFFIE, B. W. *Colonial Latin America.* Harrisburg, Pa.: Stackpole & Sons, 1945.

DOZER, DONALD M. *The Monroe Doctrine.* New York: Knopf (Borzoi Book on Latin America), 1965.

FRIEDLANDER, STANLEY L. *Labor Migration and Economic Growth: A Case Study of Puerto Rico.* Cambridge: M.I.T. Press, 1965.

GLAZER, NATHAN, and MOYNIHAN, DANIEL P. *Beyond the Melting Pot: The Negroes, Puerto Ricans, Jews, Italians and Irish of New York City.* Cambridge: M.I.T. Press, 1963.

GOODSELL, CHARLES T. *Administration of a Revolution: Executive Reforms in Puerto Rico under Governor Tugwell 1941–46.* Cambridge: Harvard University Press, 1965.

GRUBER, RUTH. *Puerto Rico: Island of Promise.* New York: Hill and Wang, 1960.

HANDLIN, OSCAR. *The Newcomers: Negroes and Puerto Ricans in a Changing Metropolis.* Cambridge: Harvard University Press, 1959.

————. *The Uprooted.* New York: Grosset and Dunlap, 1951.

HANKE, LEWIS. *The Struggle for Justice in the Conquest of America.* Philadelphia: University of Pennsylvania Press, 1949.

————. *Aristotle and the American Indians.* (Borzoi Book on Latin America.)

————. *The First Social Experiments in America.* Gloucester, Mass.: Peter Smith, 1964.

HANSON, EARL PARKER. *Puerto Rico: Ally for Progress.* Toronto: D. Van Nostrand Co., Inc., 1962.

HARING, C. H. *Spanish Empire in America.* New York: Harbinger Books, Harcourt, Brace and World, Inc., 1947.

HAUBERG, CLIFFORD A. *Economic and Social Developments in Panama 1849–1880.* (Unpublished Thesis, University of Minnesota, Minneapolis, April, 1950.)

————. *Panama and the League of Nations.* (Unpublished Thesis, University of Minnesota, Minneapolis, July, 1940.)

————. *Latin American Revolutions.* Minneapolis: T. S. Denison & Co., 1968.

HERNÁNDEZ, JOSEPH WM. "The Sociological Implications on Return Migration in Puerto Rico: An Exploratory Study." Unpublished Doctoral Thesis, University of Minnesota, 1964.

HERNANDEZ-ALVAREZ, JOSÉ. *Return Migration in Puerto Rico.* Social Science Research Center, University of Puerto Rico, 1964.

HOETINK, H. *Caribbean Race Relations: A Study of Two Variants.* New York: Oxford University Press, 1971.

HOWARD, JOHN R. *Awakening Minorities: American Indians, Mexican-Americans, Puerto Ricans.* Chicago: Aldine Publishing Co. (Transaction Book), 1970.

JOHNSON, CHALMERS. *Revolution and the Social System.* Hoover Institution Studies: 3. Stanford: Stanford University, 1964.

JONES, CLARENCE, and RAFAEL PICO. *Symposium on the Geography of Puerto Rico.* San Piedras: University of Puerto Rico Press, 1955.

LEWIS, GORDON R. *Puerto Rico: Freedom and Power in the Caribbean.* New York: MR Press, 1963.

LEWIS, OSCAR. *La Vida: A Puerto Rican Family in the Culture of Poverty–San Juan and New York.* New York: Random House, 1965.

————. *A Study of Slum Culture: Background for La Vida.* New York: Random House, 1968.

MACK, GERSTLE. *The Land Divided: A History of the Panama Canal.* New York: Alfred A. Knopf, 1944.

MALDONADO DENIS, MANUEL. *Puerto Rico: Una Interpretación Histórica-Social.* Mexico City: Editores Siglo XXI, 1969.

MATHEWS, THOMAS. *Puerto Rican Politics and the New Deal.* Gainesville: University of Florida Press, 1960.

MAYER, MILTON. *On Liberty: Man v. the State.* Center for Study of Democratic Institutions, Santa Barbara, Calif., 1969.

MILLS, C. WRIGHT, SENIOR, CLARENCE, and GOLDSEN, ROSE KOHN.

The Puerto Rican Journey: New York's Newest Migrants. New York: Harper & Bros., 1950.

MINTZ, SIDNEY W. *Worker in the Cane: A Puerto Rican Life History.* New Haven: Yale University Press, 1960.

PADILLA, ELENA. *Up From Puerto Rico.* New York: Columbia University Press, 1958.

PAGÁN, BOLIVÁR. *Historia de los Partidos Politicos Puertorriqueños (1898–1965).* Tomo I. and II. San Juan: Libreria Campos, 1959.

PAGE, HOMER. *Puerto Rico: The Quiet Revolution.* New York: Viking Press, 1964.

PEDREIRA, ANTONIO S. *Insularismo, Ensayos de Interpretación Puertorriqueña.* San Juan: Biblioteca de Autores Puertorriqueños. 2nd ed., 1942.

––––––. *Hostos: Ciudadano de América.* San Juan: Institute of Puerto Rican Culture, 1964.

PERKINS, DEXTER. *Hands Off: A History of the Monroe Doctrine.* Boston: Little, Brown & Co., 1941.

POSTMAN, NEIL (and CHARLES WEINGARTNER). *Teaching as a Subversive Activity.* New York: Delacorte Press, 1969.

RAND, CHRISTOPHER. *The Puerto Ricans.* New York: Oxford University Press, 1958.

ROSARIO, JOSÉ C. *The Development of the Puerto Rican Jíbaro and His Present Attitude Towards Society.* Monograph of the University of Puerto Rico, 1935. Series C., No. 1.

SEDA-BONILLA, EDUARDO. *Interracción Social y Personalidad en una Comunidad de Puerto Rico.* San Juan: Ediciones Juan Ponce de Léon, 1964.

SENIOR, CLARENCE. *The Puerto Ricans: Strangers—Then Neighbors.* Chicago: Quadrangle Books, 1961, 1965.

STEWARD, J. H. *Handbook of South American Indians.* Vol. 4. Washington, 1946.

THOMAS, PIRI. *Down These Mean Streets.* New York: Alfred A Knopf, 1967.

TUGWELL, REXFORD G. *The Art of Politics: As Practiced by Three Great Americans:* Franklin Delano Roosevelt, Luis Muñoz Marín, and Fiorello H. LaGuardia. New York: Doubleday & Co., 1958.

––––––. *The Stricken Land: The Story of Puerto Rico.* New York: Doubleday & Co., 1947.

VIVAS, JOSÉ LUIS. *Historia de Puerto Rico.* New York: Las Américas Publishing Co., 1962.

WAGENHEIM, KAL. *Puerto Rico: A Profile.* New York: Praeger Publishers, 1970.

WAKEFIELD, DAN. *Island in the City: Puerto Ricans in New York.* New York, Corinth, 1957.

WELLS, HENRY. *The Modernization of Puerto Rico.* (A Study of Changing Values and Institutions) Cambridge, Mass.: Harvard University Press, 1969.

PAMPHLETS AND MISCELLANEA

BADILLO, HERMAN. "Speech to the House of Representatives on May 4, 1971." New York.

—————. *Congressional Record,* June 7, 1971.

CASTAÑO, CARLOS. "The Puerto Rican Migratory Program," *Makers of America—Emergent Minorities. Encyclopaedia Britannica.* Wm. Benton, Publisher, New York, 1970, pp. 27, 28.

COMMAGER, HENRY STEELE. *The Study of History.* Charles and Merrill Books, Inc., 1966.

CORDOVA, JORGE L. "Citizenship." Puerto Rico Booklets No. 7. Office of the Commonwealth of Puerto Rico, Washington, D.C., May, 1971.

"Characteristics of Passengers who Travelled by Air Between Puerto Rico and the United States, 1958–1962," San Juan: Commonwealth of Puerto Rico, Bureau of Labor Statistics, 1958–1962.

FERRÉ, LUIS A. "Cultural Reaffirmation in the New Life." Puerto Rican Booklet Series No. 6. Office of the Commonwealth of Puerto Rico, Washington, D.C., June 1970.

FORTAS, ABE. "A Mission for Puerto Rico." Puerto Rico Booklets No. 4, Office of the Commonwealth of Puerto Rico, Washington, D.C., 1966.

HANKE, LEWIS. *All the People of the World are Men.* (James Ford Bell Lectures No. 8), University of Minnesota, Minneapolis, 1970.

ICKEN-SAFA, HELEN. "Puerto Rican Adaptation to the Urban Milieu." Latin American Institute. Reprint No. 5. State of New Jersey. New Brunswick, N.J. 08903.

MORALES CARRIÓN, ARTURO. "The Loneliness of Luis Muñoz Rivera." Puerto Rico Booklets, Series No. 1, Office of the Commonwealth of Puerto Rico, Washington, D.C., 1965.

MUÑOZ MARÍN, LUIS. "Breakthrough from Nationalism." Godkin Lectures, Harvard University, April 1959.

Office of the Commonwealth of Puerto Rico. *Puerto Rico and the U.S.A.* Washington, D.C., December 1969.

POLANCO-ABREU, SANTIAGO. "The Economic Development of Puerto Rico." Puerto Rico Booklets No. 3, Office of the Commonwealth of Puerto Rico, Washington, D.C., 1966.

Puerto Rican Revolutionary Party. *The Ideology of the Young Lords*

Party. National Headquarters, 357 Willis Avenue, Bronx, New York, 1972.

RODRÍGUEZ, CRISTÓBAL. *La República de Panamá y la Sociedad de las Naciones.* Panamá City, República de Panamá, 1929.

SCOTT, FRANKLIN D. "Emigration and Immigration" (2nd ed.). Pub. No. 51. Service Center for Teachers of History. American Historical Association, 1963. Baltimore: Waverly Press.

SENIOR, CLARENCE, and WATKINS, DONALD O. "Toward a Balance Sheet of Puerto Rican Migration." Status of Puerto Rico Selected Background Studies prepared for the United States-Puerto Rico Commission on the Status of Puerto Rico. Hearings, Senate Document No. 108, 1966.

"The Status of Puerto Rico." Puerto Rican Booklet Series No. 5. *Report of the U.S.-Puerto Rican Commission for the Study of the Status of Puerto Rico.* Office of the Commonwealth of Puerto Rico, Washington, D.C., 1967.

VILELLA, ROBERTO SANCHEZ. "The Story of Puerto Rico." Puerto Rico Booklets Series No. 2. Office of the Commonwealth of Puerto Rico, Washington, D.C., 1965.

PERIODICALS AND NEWS ITEMS

"Arnie Has the Plane, Chi Chi the Gas." *Minneapolis Tribune.* (July 20, 1971), 1 C.

BROWNING, FRANK. "From Rumble to Revolution: The Young Lords." *Ramparts.* (Oct. 1970), 19–25.

FITZPATRICK, JOSEPH P. "Puerto Ricans in Perspective: The Meaning of Migration to the Mainland." *International Migration Review.* II (Spring, 1968), 7–19.

––––––. "Attitudes of Puerto Ricans Toward Color." *American Catholic Sociological Review.* II (No. 3, Fall, 1959), 219–33.

––––––. "The Intermarriage of Puerto Ricans in New York City." *American Journal of Sociology.* LXXI (Jan. 1966), 395–406.

GOODSELL, CHARLES T. "Puerto Rico Moves Forward." *Current History,* December 1966, 321–26.

HAUBERG, C. A. "Panama: Pro Mundi Beneficia." *Current History,* April 1957.

HERNÁNDEZ-ALVAREZ, JOSÉ. "Migration, Return and Development in Puerto Rico." *Economic Development and Cultural Change.* XVI (July, 1968), 574–87.

––––––. "The Movement and Settlement of Puerto Rican Migrants Within the United States, 1950–1960." *International Migration Review.* II (Spring, 1968), 40–51.

"House of Studies." (Taken from *U.S. Journal*, San Juan, Puerto Rico) in *The New Yorker*, Feb. 14, 1960.

"Identity Crisis." *Newsweek*, Jan. 19, 1970.

JENKINS, DAN. *Sports Illustrated*. XXI (Aug. 10, 1964), 34–35.

"Job Plan Helpful to Puerto Ricans." *New York Times*. (June 1, 1971), pp. 31–32.

KANTROWITZ, NATHAN. "Social Mobility of Puerto Ricans: Education, Occupation, and Income Changes among Children of Migrants, New York—1950–1960." *International Migration Review*. II (Spring, 1968), 53–71.

LEWIS, OSCAR. "One Can Suffer Anywhere." *Harper's*, May 1969.

LIDIN, HAROLD J. "Bombs, Bullets, Scribblings." *San Juan Star*. San Juan, Puerto Rico, Nov. 16, 1959.

LOPEZ, LILLIAN. "New York: The South Bronx Project." *Wilson Library Bulletin* (Mar., 1970), 757–59.

MACISCO, JOHN J. "The Assimilation of the Puerto Ricans on the Mainland: A Socio-Demographic Approach." *International Migration Review*, II (Spring, 1968), 21–38.

MEYERS, GEORGE. "Migration and Modernization in Puerto Rico, 1950–1960." *Social and Economic Studies*. XVI (Dec. 1967), 425–31.

MEYERSON, MICHAEL. "Puerto Rico: Our Backyard Colony." *Ramparts* (June 1970), 51.

MINTZ, SIDNEY. "Puerto Rican Emigration: A Threefold Comparison." *Social and Economic Studies*. IV (Dec. 1955), 311–25.

MORALES CARRIÓN, ARTURO. "What is a Puerto Rican?" *The Island Times*. San Juan, Puerto Rico, Nov. 24, 1961.

MUÑOZ MARÍN, LUIS. "The Sad Case of Puerto Rico." *The American Magazine*. February 1929, 136–41.

"People in Sports." *Minneapolis Tribune*. July 21, 1971, 3 C.

PRATT, J. H. "Origins of Manifest Destiny." *American Historical Review*, Vol. 32, pp. 795–98.

STONE, LEROY. "Population Redistribution and Economic Development in Puerto Rico, 1950–1960." *Social and Economic Studies*. XIV (Sept. 1965), 264–71.

"The Puerto Ricans." *Newsweek*. LXXV June 15, 1970, 92–93.

The Rican (Revista de pensamiento contemporáneo puertorriqueño) Published quarterly. P.O. Box 11039, Chicago. Conferences and Correspondence with Various Puerto Ricans, including Herman Badillo and Jorge Cordova.

Index

ABOUT THE AUTHOR

Clifford A. Hauberg began teaching Latin American history in the Canal Zone schools (Panama) in the early 1940s. He has since taught Latin American history at the University of Wisconsin (summer sessions 1956, 1964) and at St. Olaf College from 1947 to the present. He also served as chairman of the History Department 1969-1971 at St. Olaf. He was visiting professor at the University of Panama during the summer session of 1954, and for the last four years he has taught an interim course at CIDOC (Centro Intercultural de Documentacion), Cuernavaca, Mexico.

Dr. Hauberg has served as consultant and has been the recipient of several grants including the Social Science Research Grant 1952-53. As a result he has traveled extensively throughout Latin America, including a trip to South America in 1969 and a summer sojourn in Bolivia as counselor for SPAN (Student Project for Amity Among Nations) sponsored by the University of Minnesota.

Dr. Hauberg did his graduate work at the University of Minnesota, where he also served as assistant and instructor in the History Department, and received his Ph.D. in 1950. He has published articles in encyclopedias, newspapers, as well as in educational and historical journals.